Courage for Survival

The Autobiography of Aristea Pettis

ISBN: 1493726528
ISBN-13: 978-1493726523

I dedicate this book to my daughter, Marie, who inspired me to write my story.

And

In loving memory of my husband Floyd with whom we spent sixty years together, side by side. For his love, support, hard work, and dedication to his family, church community, and to me his wife— I am truly blessed.

Front Cover: At age 9, pictured with my mother and brothers, Michael, 7, and
Elefterios, 5

CONTENTS

ACKNOWLEDGMENTS

I never thought I would write my story (by write I mean literally handwrite), especially considering that English is my second language. It has been many years since I owned a typewriter and I never jumped into the world of computers. I had many people assist me in this journey, all of whom I am ever so thankful to for their assistance.

I want to especially thank Paul Contos, who gave me the idea and encouragement to attend the seniors writing class through The Metropolitan Adult Education program. I would also like to thank my instructor, Ann Thompson, and all of the students who gave me feedback and encouragement on a weekly basis. A very special thank you to a friend I made in the class, Pauline Chand, who assisted me in typing, editing, and researching. Most importantly I would like to thank her for her encouragement and friendship. Also her husband Norm Chand who changed all of my old photos into a digital format.

Thank you to those who assisted me by typing some of the pages of my book: Judith Guardino, Mark Judge, Ann Halversen, and Andy Leach.

Lastly, I would like to thank my children for their love, support, and assistance: Tony Pettis, George Pettis and David Pettis. A very special thank you to my daughter, Maria, who not only inspired me, but also spent countless hours typing, editing, researching, and questioning me to bring out the events of my life as I truly experienced them, which was often times difficult for me to relive. I also want to remember my grandchildren and thank them for their love and support: Tonya Foster, Nicole Sloan, Erik Pettis, Brian Pettis, Paul Petrogeorge, and Niko Petrogeorge. Thank you everyone. You all made the dream of writing my story become a reality.

ABOUT CRETE

The Island of Crete was a place of early European civilization. They early civilizations on Crete were forerunners in sanitation, engineering, and other technological innovations. The famous palace of Knossos is in Crete, where the oldest royal throne in Europe was established. The early Cretans were not only lovers of architecture and man-made beauty but also natural beauty. This is evident by the elaborate decorations of nature that are on many of their artistic creations. They were also lovers of sports and other gentile pursuits that people still enjoy to this day. The people of Crete were true pioneers of civilization, flourishing at the very dawn of refinement and sophistication.

MOHOS

My mother was in her floral cotton dress in the kitchen frying *tiganites* (johnnycakes). She made enough for us to snack on all day. This is my earliest memory of my beloved home in the village of *Mohos*. I was born in Mohos, which is about thirty-five kilometers east of Iraklion, the largest city on the island of Crete in Greece. At that time, Mohos had about three thousand people.

Many of the people in our town had visited the city of Iraklion, although transportation was rarely available. The roads were full of holes, which turned to mud when it rained, making travel even more difficult. My mother's brother, Uncle Nicholas, often traveled to Iraklion by bus or, when there was no bus service, by donkey.

Uncle Nicholas was a salesman and visited storeowners to take orders and deliver goods. He supplied them with flour, beans, olive oil, and wine. Occasionally, he would also provide lamb or pork if it was available. When

Uncle Nicholas would return from the city, he would visit my parents and end up staying for dinner. He would sit for hours telling stories about all the places he visited and about all the things that had impressed him in Iraklion.

"Everything in the city is beautiful," he told us. He especially admired the electric lights that lit up the city at night. He loved the city life. Uncle Nicholas especially liked to talk about the old city of Knossos where the first European civilization was born in 3500 BCE. Knossos was the center of the Minoan civilization. The luxurious Palace of Knossos was filled with various scenes painted on the walls that depicted dolphins, fish, cats, vases, athletes doing acrobatics, and many other figures.

I remember sitting close to Uncle Nicholas, becoming enthralled while listening to him tell us fascinating stories. I became so excited! How I wished I could go to the big city of Iraklion to see all the wonderful places of which he spoke. I did not know then that my family would move there two years later.

LIFE IN THE VILLAGE

Life in Mohos was simple and quiet. There were no cars, telephones, or police sirens to awaken us at night. We lived on the southern end of town and did not even get the noise of early morning traffic as everyone traveled north to work herding their sheep, goats, and donkeys. It was mostly peaceful except for when the rooster crowed or the donkey brayed.

Our home, like most of the others in the village, was built of stone, as wood was scarce. Mother told me that my grandfather, who was a stonemason built our house. An eight-foot wall surrounded it and a large courtyard greeted you when you entered. Mother had planters filled with geraniums, gardenias, sweet basil, and jasmine in the courtyard, causing the entire area to smell sweet all summer long.

My grandfather had built our house to last. A circular stone arch supported the living room. To the left of the living room, three steps down, was a ten by fourteen foot storage room that housed huge clay jars, which were about four feet high and thirty inches in diameter. These were used to store olive oil, flour, legumes and various grains.

Seven steps up from the storage room was my parents' bedroom. Next to their room was a bedroom that my two brothers shared. I slept on a sofa in the living room. The house was shaped like the letter L. The kitchen was on the left corner and it had a large window that looked out onto the courtyard. I remember looking out this window into the courtyard every day, waiting for my parents to come home from working in the fields where they cultivated grapes or picking olives. My brothers and I often stayed home alone while my parents worked. Occasionally our Uncle Nicholas, who lived nearby, would look after us. He often arrived with a bowlful of homemade buttermilk that we loved to eat with *paximathi* (biscotti).

Every morning, my parents would rise at dawn. Mother began each day by lighting the fireplace and preparing our breakfast of tea, toast, and cheese. She would then prepare sandwiches for our lunch and place them in a basket. Some days she would promise to bring us candy if we were good. When this happened it was a very rare treat, so my brothers and I tried to be on our best behavior all day.

Most days were very long for us children. At five years old, I was the oldest of my siblings so it was my job to watch over my brothers, Michael, three, and Eleftherios, a year old. We would tire ourselves out playing hide-and-

seek and jump rope, which would culminate in us falling
asleep for an afternoon nap. When we woke up, we would
look out the window and know by the shadow of the sun
on the wall that it was almost time for our parents to come
home from the fields. We would stand by the window and
listen for the sound of the donkey's bray or its hooves on
the cobblestones. Soon, we would hear the donkey leading
the way for the goats and our parents walking behind.

"Mother, mother," we shouted, happy to have her
home again. After giving us each a big hug and a piece of
candy she lit the fire and started to prepare dinner. All of
our hugs came from Mother. Father was not the type to
hug or cuddle but we knew by his actions that he loved us.
It was during the winter months that we had the best times
with my father. He loved to play games and tell us stories
that we loved to hear. He would roast garbanzo beans for
us to munch on as he told us about Ali Baba and the forty
thieves. We sat spellbound through the whole story,
especially when he told us the part when the rock was
removed from the entrance of the cave by saying the magic
words, *open sesame.* We enjoyed trying to beat him in
checkers, although we were never able to do so.

My childhood memories are happy memories. That
is not to say that life in Mohos was easy. My parents
worked hard to provide the basic necessities: food,
clothing, and shelter. They gave us the gift of pride in
ourselves and our heritage, and most importantly, we knew
we were loved.

WINTER EVENINGS

Now in my old age, I gaze at a flickering candle and I can still recall winter nights in Mohos when the neighborhood women gathered in our house to embroider. They each carried their own *lychnary* (oil lamp) and would hang it on a stand against the wall as they entered the house. I recall the glimmer of the lamplight. It grew brighter as first one, and then another, and another lamp was added to the stand, and soon the room was filled with a soft glow. The women worked together embroidering pillowcases, bed sheets, tablecloths, and many other articles. They liked to tell jokes and laugh at their own cleverness as they competed with one another to tell the best jokes. Embroidery and laughter made the winter months pass faster.

While the women worked I played with my friends, Antonia and Georgia. We played with dolls that my mother made from rags and the boys played jacks with pebbles gathered from the seashore. Sometimes we played checkers. Our checkerboard was drawn on cardboard and we used either stones or colored legumes for the checkers.

In Mohos we were always surrounded with people. In town we had many friends and relatives who were close, just like a big family. We all helped each other. If Mother was sick everybody in the neighborhood knew it. Women would bring us chicken soup and squash casserole and take care of us children.

The neighbors watched over each other's children often. If we misbehaved while our parents were away, our neighbors would reprimand us. It was this correction, combined with the care and love they showed us that made us respect their discipline and have obedience. I remember playing on the street with the neighborhood children when one of the boys threw a rock that hit me on the leg. His mother made him carry my books to school for a week as punishment. I learned that there was always someone watching out for me.

My Yiayia's lychnary, which now rests on my fireplace in California

GATHERIN IN THE TOWN SQUARE

Church days were very special for my brothers and I. After the services were over, we would meet our friends and relatives at the *plateia* (town square), which was one of our favorite places. The plateia was pleasant, as the thick green-leafed mulberry trees that surrounded it offered shade during the hot summer months. Coffee shops and restaurants with tables and chairs surrounded the plateia, offering people a place to gather and visit. I can remember spring and summer when the tables were covered with blue and white checked tablecloths and adorned with vases filled with snow-white jasmine. A gentle breeze would often carry the scent of the jasmine, pleasantly filling the air of our cherished plateia. The restaurant owners would frequently barbeque lamb shish kabobs and serve them with french fries.

Occasionally, when my parents had the money, they would order lunch for us. If it happened to be someone's name day (especially a man) he might hire two or three musicians to play *bouzoukia* (Greek stringed instrument) or the Cretan *lyra* (violin played vertically on the knee). As was the custom, the man whose name day it was would also buy food and refreshments for everyone present. Young and old would celebrate by dancing traditional dances until midnight or the early hours of the next morning.

Our plateia was a special place for us because it had a water well that provided drinking water for the residents in the village, as no one had running water in their homes. At the top of the well was a horizontal wheel that was connected to a pipe that is turned by a donkey. The pipe is connected from the wheel to the donkey. As the donkey walks around the well, water runs into a pipe and fills earthen jugs that women brought from home. I recall that sometimes my father would go with the donkey to fill the jugs and bring them home. My brothers, friends, and I enjoyed chasing each other around the well.

Next to the well was a large, wooden trough that was usually full of water for cattle to drink. Every evening, after the day's work was done, the farmers would bring their animals to drink water beside the well.

MY FATHER'S LIFE ON THE FAMILY FARM

Many of the people in the village made their living by farming. In most cases, farmers would divide their fields into narrow strips so that when a parent would die the property could easily be separated among the children. This method of land division would often times result in people owning strips of land that were not near each other. Farmers would have to waste valuable time traveling between their various pieces of land. Often times my father would talk to other farmers in an effort to exchange property in order to have more land in one place.

My father worked hard to cultivate the orchards. He grew apples, pears, and peaches, but grapes were his specialty. He knew how to prune and graft the vines to create other varieties of the fruit. He was also an expert winemaker.

My father was a handsome man, six feet tall, and strong. As a result of working outdoors his entire life he had weathered features, which made him good-looking. He had a gift for remembering the stories he read, including a popular book, *Erotokritos*, written by a Cretan author, Vikentios Kornaros. I still have my father's copy of this book. It is a romantic narrative poem that tells a love story between a princess and a young man whose father was the advisor to the King of Athens in the sixteen century. The young man would pretend to visit his father so that he could see the princess. When the king found out about all this, he exiled the young man to a foreign land. My father could recite from memory hundreds of pages of this fascinating story. When he worked with his friends in the vineyards they would beg him to recite this beautiful love story.

My Father's friends loved to hear him recite the *Erotokritos*

THE KAFENIO AND GENERAL STORE

I remember a warm day in February when my father returned from the *kafenio* (coffee shop). He would go there often to have his coffee and read the newspaper. News was very important to him, especially government and politics, which were discussed in great detail and with passion between my father and his friends. They had a lot of fun trying to outsmart each other.

When he returned home from the kafenio that one morning, Mother said, "You returned just in time. Breakfast is ready. I made your favorite, *tiganites* with honey syrup, cinnamon, and nuts on top."

Father told us, "I have something to show you. I want you to look down the street at that beautiful tree in full bloom." It was an almond tree covered in clusters of snow-white blossoms with pink centers. There it stood, like a bride all dressed in white. Father told us that when an almond tree is in full bloom it is an indication that spring is just around the corner.

After breakfast, he decided that we would all go

shopping together at the general store. Saturday was our usual shopping day. My parents, brothers, and I went to the general store at the plaza. The store was whitewashed on the outside and trimmed with green painted window frames and had a green wooden door. It had a large glass window that displayed various materials such as wool, cotton, and linen. We could also see beautiful blankets, tablecloths, and other handmade crafts. Inside the store, one could smell various aromas coming from glass jars filled with candy and spices that were displayed on shelves. Many of the glass jars contained colorful candy that was pleasant to the eye and to one's palate. Mother's favorite things to shop for were knitting yarn and embroidery thread. She did a lot of needlework on pillowcases, doilies, tablecloths, and many other projects. The general store supplied the villagers with hardware such as shovels, picks, oxen pliers, saws, beads, clothing, and threads in a variety of qualities and colors.

On this particular day, besides purchasing supplies for the early spring planting, as a special treat Father bought us some hard candy– cinnamon, lemon and, peppermint. But it was the custom necklaces and bracelets hanging inside the vitrine that took my attention. I didn't dare ask my parents to buy any of them because I knew they had very little money and they would always buy what they needed most. Just the same, I had a lot of fun going to the general store with my parents.

MY MOTHER

My mother, Maria, was born in Mohos in January of 1903. She had one sister, Kaliope, and three brothers, George, Michael, and Nicholas. Mother had huge hazel eyes and shoulder length hair that was chestnut with sunny highlights. When she walked through the town to get water from the well young men would stop to admire her.

Mother was an excellent cook and despite helping my father in the fields all day, she still prepared a full dinner for us when she came home. We did not eat very much meat in those days so it was very special when it was served. My mother would normally fix us vegetable stew that was made with string beans, zucchini, potatoes, fresh tomatoes, onions, and parsley. We would eat a lot of lentils and various types of beans either in the form of soup or combined with rice. We would also have either white cabbage salad or *horiatiki salata* (village salad) made with ripe summer tomatoes, cucumbers, green onions, bell peppers, fresh parsley, black olives, and feta cheese. It was always served with homemade bread. Another favorite was stewed grape or cabbage leaves stuffed with rice, onions, and herbs. Small, fried fish were also occasionally served. French fries cooked in olive oil and topped off with sea salt was another favorite food. My mother made the most delicious spaghetti sauce using fresh tomatoes, onion, garlic, bay leafs, and a couple of tablespoons of red wine. When we poured this sauce over spaghetti and added a little grated, homemade cheese, we were set for life! How yummy it was!

Water was the main beverage for our family but Mom and Dad usually had a glass of homemade wine with meals. Greek coffee was served on special occasions or when guests came to visit. Usually the only dessert we ever had was whatever fresh fruit was available according to the season. In the winter we had quince, pomegranate, oranges, tangerines, winter pears, and apples. The summer season brought us sun-kissed fruit beginning with loquats that were followed by an abundance of honeydew melons, cantaloupe, grapes of all kinds, and sweet, juicy watermelon. Best of all, we had the most wonderful variety of mouth-watering red and white figs. For a very special treat Mother would buy cherries to make into a preserve that could be served to guests who came to visit. These preserves were served in a small spoon on small plates. Of course we children would get some too by sneaking a little bit for ourselves.

In addition to feeding us so well Mother also made our clothes. Sometimes the seams did not fit correctly, as Mother did not have a sewing machine, but she did her best. She never complained about anything, making it all look effortless. That was her gift to us. Only our Sunday clothes were made by a seamstress. We were always glad to have something new and professionally sewn to wear, even if it was only once a year. We went barefoot during most of the summer months so that we could save our shoes for church or for attending weddings or baptisms.

Like most people in those days, my parents had high standards for us children: near perfect grades, impressive athletic ability, complete integrity, and high morality. As it turned out, my brothers and I received good grades in school. As rigid as my mother seemed to be at times, it was my father who was the real perfectionist, the one who expected it all from his children and from his wife. It was my father who put the pressure on all of us. My mother always tried her hardest to make a happy home for all of us and she succeeded. In spite of having very little we were always happy.

A DAY IN THE FIELDS

My parents arose before sunrise. My mother lit the fireplace and I was woken by the sound and smell of dry sage and thyme crackling in the fire. Lighting the fire to prepare breakfast was Mother's first chore every morning. Sometimes my brothers and I did not wake up until the smell of pancakes reached our noses.

I remember one day in April it was still cold in the morning and the warmth of the fire felt good to our hands. After breakfast Mother said, "You can come to work in the fields with us today, but you must dress warmly." She prepared tahini (sesame butter) sandwiches with honey to take for lunch and placed them in a beautiful basket that my grandmother made from golden colored wheat stalks.

We were so excited to go with my parents that we jumped up and down with joy. We helped Mother carry what she needed to the courtyard so that Father could load the donkey. When everything was loaded, Father checked to make sure we had water and food for the day as well as the seeds for planting, especially the whole-wheat seeds, as this was the season to plant summer wheat. We took our young milking goat along to let her graze while my parents worked. Mother said, "You children can watch the goat."

We left home and started walking on the narrow cobblestone streets before the sun came up. On the way we met a lot of our neighbors along with their goats, cows, and sheep. It was exciting, all of us going to our fields to plant wheat, oats, and barley. The sun began to rise and the warmth felt good to my body. There were no clouds in the sky and there was not even a hint of morning dew upon the air; the day was gorgeous.

Walking on the trail was slow, as it was very rough and full of rocks. We walked and walked for what seemed like hours, though in actuality it was about an hour. We enjoyed the sights around us. We saw birds flying happily from tree to tree and watched robins building their nests. A wild rabbit hopped up from behind the bushes and scared us. Anemone grew among the rocks in warm shades of yellow, orange, pink, red, and white. The sweet aroma of herbs filled the air as we passed wild shrubs of rosemary, sage, oregano, and thyme.

Finally, we arrived at our property. Father unloaded the food and supplies while Mother hung the basket of food on a tree branch and put the water jug by the trunk of the tree so that it would be easy for us children to get a drink whenever we were thirsty. Father hitched the plow to the donkey and slowly began to plow the ground while Mother walked behind him and planted the wheat seeds.

My brothers and I watched the goat graze while we

picked wild flowers and made a wreath from willow branches with the wild flowers tied onto it. When we returned home we hung it on the front door to dry so that we could use it for a future event.

That evening, after dinner, Uncle Nicholas came to visit us bringing a bag of chestnuts and some candy. He sat down on a bench close to the fireplace and roasted the chestnuts while he told us stories that he made up as he went along. It was the perfect ending to another wonderful day in Mohos.

CHURCH ON SUNDAYS

The village of Mohos had two churches. The one church, Saint George, was in the northern part of the village. The other church on the lower end of the plateia was named *Panagia* (Virgin Mary) and most of the people who lived in the lower part of the town, like us, would attend church services there.

Mother would prepare us for church by giving each of us a bath on Saturday evenings. We would take turns standing in a metal tub while she soaped our bodies with olive oil soap and a cloth rag. She would rinse the soap off of our bodies by pouring warm water over our heads from a huge black kettle that she had heated the water in. It always felt refreshing to have our hair washed and clean.

On Sunday morning Mother always made sure that we wore clean clothes to church. As the *Panagia* church was close to our home, Mother, my brothers, and I would walk there. Early Sunday morning the sound of bells would ripple through the air, landing on our ears and filling our hearts with joy. This was how we were called to make our stroll toward the sacred place in which we worshipped God. As we made our way to *Panagia,* the fragrant aroma of incense coming from the neighbors' homes would fill the air, as it was customary for people to incense their homes before going to church. As a child it felt so peaceful to be in church praying with my mother. It felt very special to be close to God and to obey the Ten Commandments that our teachers taught us in school.

Sundays were very special for us children for another reason besides church. After the services were over, we would go to meet our friends and relatives at the plateia, which was one of our favorite places. We enjoyed spending time there, playing together with our friends.

My father seldom went to church. Instead, he would visit the kafenio and spend the morning drinking coffee and playing cards with his friends. He went to church about four times a year: Christmas, New Year, Easter, and the fifteenth day of August, which was the celebration of our church's name day. We all wished that he would go to church more but that was just wishful thing. Nevertheless, we all enjoyed our peaceful and happy Sundays in Mohos.

OUR EASTER CELEBRATION

Easter is the most important religious festival for the Greek Orthodox people. During Holy Week, we would faithfully fast from meat and dairy products (we usually didn't have money to buy meat anyway). The women were busy coloring eggs red and baking traditional Greek *koulourakia* and *kourabiedes* cookies, in addition to sweet Easter bread with a red egg in the middle of a round loaf. They would bake the bread in an outdoor stone oven, which caused the whole town to be filled with the aroma of baking goodies.

Meanwhile, the boys in the town went to the hills to gather sagebrush. Every day during Holy Week they would bring enough brush into the platia to make a huge pile. They attached a rag effigy of Judas to a broomstick and placed it on top of the pile, ready to be set alight.

When Holy Friday evening arrived we went to church with Mother. The services were so long it seemed as though we stood there for hours. The church had no pews.

After a while I would drop to the multi-colored ceramic floor and go to sleep on my mother's brown winter coat.

The women stood on the left side of the church with their children and the men stood on the right with the boys older than sixteen. On each side of the church, against the walls, there were a few *stasithia* for the older people to sit upon. *Stasithia* are wooden stands with a moveable seat that folds up or down on hinges. The seat can be folded down if a person wants to sit or lifted up if one wants to stand. These carved wooden stands are about four feet tall and one and a half feet deep. There are high arms to rest on when in the standing position. Some *stasithia* have simple designs while others are intricately carved.

Mother would rouse us from our sleep when the priest came out of the altar the chant the traditional Lamentation hymn while standing in front of the *kouvouklion.* The *kouvouklion* represents the tomb of Jesus Christ. It is an intricately hand-carved wooden table with an elaborate dome held up by four pillars that rest on the corners of a table. The carved design displays peacocks or grapevines: symbols of Christ and the Resurrection. On Holy Friday morning the women decorate the *kouvouklion* with freshly cut honeysuckle, jasmine, lilies, and carnations. Inside the tomb is a red velvet cloth in the Byzantine iconographic style on which Christ is depicted lying with his hands across his chest as if dead in the tomb. The cloth, called the *epitaphios,* is beautifully decorated with embroidery of gold, silver, and various other colored threads and beadwork.

The hymns of the Lamentations speak of the paradox of how the creator of life lies dead in the tomb. From the hymns we hear the voice of the Virgin Mary weeping for her son, asking the perplexing questions, and speaking of Jesus revealing himself as the Christ through his resurrection. There is no way to describe the beautiful Byzantine melodies that accompany the lyrics, they stir the soul like the wind stirs the branches of a tree before a storm and then rain comes to subdue the dryness of the earth. These hymns are what we call joyful-sadness. We are saddened because we lament the sufferings of our beloved Lord and yet joyful because we know that the chains of death cannot contain the creator of life.

The apex of the Holy Friday service is a procession that takes place outside the church. The altar boys lead the procession carrying the cross, candles, fans, and banners. They are followed four men who carry the *epitaphion* on their shoulders. Coming behind the *epitaphion* is the priest and then the people, each of whom carries a lit candle that illuminates their joyful faces.

As we proceeded out the front door of the church into the cool night, the beauty of the heavens above, thick with stars, awed us. The candles we carried seemed to mirror the starlit night sky. The procession proceeded around the church as we gently sang, "Holy God, Holy Mighty, Holy Immortal have mercy on us."

During this procession the priest makes three stops at each side of the church where he sings a phrase of litanies asking God for peace in the world, temperate

seasons, forgiveness of sins, and for help in living a life of
repentance and holiness. He asks for the Holy Spirit to
guide the leaders of the church. In larger cities like Iraklion,
where there were as many as twenty churches, there would
be twenty *kouvouklion* in the streets, each with a throng of
people carrying candles and following in a funeral-like
procession.

On Holy Saturday we would all take an afternoon
nap and have a light lunch when we woke up. Around
eleven at night we would leave for church for the midnight
Paschal Resurrection service. At midnight the priest comes
out from the altar with a large candle in his hand. He makes
the sign of the cross and chants, "Come receive the light."
One by one the worshippers light their candles until the
entire church is illuminated.

My breath would be taken away as I saw the candles
being lit, anticipating being able to utter for the first time
since last year, as if it were the first time ever, *Christ is risen!*
We would process outside the church to hear the priest
read the gospel about the resurrection of Christ. After the
reading was finished the priest would proclaim, "Christ is
risen!" and we would all sing the resurrection hymn with
joyful exuberance. We would then go back inside the
church where the priest began the Divine Liturgy.

We finish the service around one-thirty in the
morning and at the end we each received a red egg that has
been blessed by the priest. On Holy Thursday, the women
prepared the eggs. The colored egg represents the sealed
tomb of Jesus. They are colored red as a symbol of the

blood he shed on the cross. People engage in contests by holding their eggs with the pointed ends facing up. One person hits another's egg while emphatically saying *Christ is Risen!* The other responds by saying *Truly His is Risen!* One of the eggs cracks, which symbolizes Christ's resurrection from the tomb. The person whose egg remains unbroken receives good luck for the year.

After the church service the people proceed out into the square as the church bells ring and fireworks go off. The boys light the huge pile of sagebrush they formed and the flames engulf Judas. The men busy themselves serving *magiritsa*, a traditional Easter lamb soup.

The celebration continues early Sunday morning when the men go to the plaza to build a fire on a big spit. They begin to roast lambs for everyone in the village, including the visitors. The women prepare vegetable dishes, salads, more Easter eggs, sweet braided Easter bread, and various kinds of fruit such as loquats, tangerines, and pomegranates. The tables are richly laden. Everyone enjoys the feast after the long fast. The children play games while the adults talk, dance, and continue to joyously wish each other *Christ is risen!* To the answer, *"Truly He is risen!"*

THRESHING TIME

June and July was the time to harvest wheat. My
father inspected the wheat fields often and when they were
golden brown he knew that the time was right for harvest.
He would begin by sharpening the sickles and preparing the
necessary equipment for harvesting. He would speak with
neighbors and friends to set a date for those who would
help him begin the harvest. In return for their help my
father would help them harvest their wheat.

My mother would awaken us early while the sky was
still dark. She would gently shake our arms saying, "Get up!
The hour to arise has come, my children." My mother,
brothers, and I got ready. We went out the gate of our
front courtyard to join my father and the relatives and
neighbors. It was like a parade as we started down the
rocky, dirt road. First came the donkeys saddled with
supplies, followed by the baahing goats, their neck bells
clanging. What a beautiful sight it was! The fresh early
morning air was filled with the scent of wild mountain sage,
thyme, oregano, and the Daphne flowers.

When we arrived at the field, each person helped with a specific task. There was a certain hum about the process. The children helped by pouring water from clay water jugs into tin cups that we carefully carried to the workers for their refreshment. Other children, along with the women, gathered the wheat that the men cut into small bundles. Father tied the small bundles together into an even larger bundle using rope made from willow branches.

Speaking of humming, the laborers worked together with great enthusiasm, reaping the grain with sickles as they sang both old and new songs. In this manner the work got done faster and seemed less tiring. The scent of the freshly harvested wheat brought to my mind the fresh baked bread that would come from it.

Around ten in the morning, we would take a half-hour break. We would sit on blankets spread out under the shade of olive trees and pull from our wool satchels some bread, feta cheese, and fresh tomatoes to snack on. The grapes were just beginning to ripen, so we enjoyed some of these as well, plucking them right off the nearby vines. A watermelon patch was close by and we enjoyed the sweet juicy flavor of freshly cut melon.

After our break we once again began carrying water to the workers, continuously going back and forth. The locusts, or perhaps crickets, began to chirp furiously as the temperature approached ninety degrees. Everybody got tired and hungry and stopped again to take a break for lunch.

A few months before the harvest, Father had built a

bamboo shed in anticipation of our need for shelter from the burning noon sun. We gathered inside the shed tired and hungry for the noonday meal. My mother put out a spread of *horiatiki* salad made of cucumbers, tomatoes, green onions, and feta with olives on the side. We would dip our bread in the salad bowl to soak up the dark green olive oil mingled with the red juice of the fresh cut tomatoes at the bottom. I can taste it now! There would be more watermelon, and for a special treat mother had prepared some *kalitsounia*, fried dough filled with sweetened cheese that sometimes included fresh mint. We ate with gusto!

After eating, everyone would rest for one hour and then resume their routines again. As the bundles of wheat were created, Father would load them onto the donkey a few at a time and walk them to the area where the wheat would be threshed. Here he would unload the bundles and stand three of them together with the heads of wheat pointing up at the sky. He would go back and forth all afternoon until dark. At sunset we would reassemble our parade of harvesters, donkeys, and goats and return home a little more quietly over the rocky road, as we were all so tired that no one had much to say. We just wanted to go home to have dinner and rest for the next day's work.

A few weeks after the wheat was harvested, we were ready to do the threshing. Before the harvest began father prepared an earthen circle fifty feet in circumference on the property we owned near the town. The circle was well packed beforehand and left to dry like cement. This *aloni* (threshing floor) was not too far from our house. Father would take some of the wheat and spread it into the circle, ready to be threshed. He would then yoke two cows or donkeys together that would pull a board behind them connected to the yoke. The board had flint stones driven into the bottom. The animals go around and around over the stems of the wheat with the stone separating the heads from the stalks.

There was a seat built on the board for the children to have fun taking turns sitting there going around like a merry-go-round. When the heads have been separated from the stalk, the wheat is gathered into a huge pile. When there is a favorable wind the wheat is tossed into the air and the chaff is separated from the head, the lighter chaff is blown away and the wheat falls again in a pile. My father would come and shovel the wheat into a burlap sack and my mother and I would take the wheat to the mill to have it ground. My Uncle Nicholas offered to come along to help us while father went to another village to sell a young goat.

We started our journey to the mill in the cool of the early morning. We began slowly climbing the rocky trail up a very steep hill. Most of the windmills were purposely built on an open hill to take advantage of the wind power available there. It takes a strong breeze to make the wind sails go around. When the wind blows the mill works night and day. We began to feel tired after walking for just one hour. The sun was beginning to feel hot on our backs. Uncle Nicholas suggested that we take a short rest to have a drink of water under a mulberry tree growing along the trail. He said we would arrive at the mill in another twenty minutes.

Once we arrived people were already in line waiting for their turn. When our turn came, I watched with great curiosity, trying to find out how the wheels turned. For me the windmill was a wondrous invention. It was my first time seeing a mill at work. I loved the smell of the fresh milled flour falling into the cotton sack from the mouth of the chute. We were so glad to have our wheat ground into flour.

Late in the afternoon when we arrived home from the mill, Mother decided to make bread without yeast, as it takes less time. She placed some of the freshly ground flour we brought from the mill into a mixing bowl. To the flour she added oil, salt, and water and then kneaded the mixture into stiff dough. Then she flattened the dough into one-inch thick squares and cooked it in a frying pan over a medium fire. She had to turn it often so it wouldn't burn. It took about twenty minutes to cook. Mother's bread tasted so delicious with bean soup. We ate it with great appetite and enjoyed having Uncle Nicholas with us. We asked him if he would tell us a story after dinner. He smiled, "I think I have one."

SPRINGTIME

One of the springtime activities I recall is washing our blankets. Mother always washed our clothing and heavy woolen blankets by hand. Each spring, Mother would carry our blankets to a lake about four miles away and hand wash them with soap that she made from olive oil and ashes. After washing the blankets she would hang them over tree branches to dry.

While she did this, we children played by the lake, keeping a careful eye out for water snakes, which were so plentiful. After the blankets had dried Mother folded them and we carried them home. We then took an afternoon nap, enjoying our freshly washed blankets.

I remember one such spring washing day when, after dinner, my friends, Antonia and Georgia, came to visit. They said that that evening was the time to celebrate May Day. We made wreaths out of fresh flowers and hung them on the door where they would dry and decorate the door all summer. At the end of August, on the eve before the feast day when we remember the beheading of Saint John the Baptist, we would light small bonfires to burn the May Day wreaths. Children and grownups alike would take turns jumping over the small fires, competing to see who could jump the furthest. Almost every neighborhood had a bonfire and the whole town would be illuminated.

A COW'S HEAD AND DANDELION GREENS

My father enjoyed traveling and was often gone for a week or more at a time. He loved the city life and was always telling Mother, "I am tired of the farming life. I wish we could sell everything and move to the city where I can make a living more easily and life would be more comfortable for all of us."

His return from one of those trips is vivid in my mind. He came home with a cow's head. He broke it into four pieces with an axe and gave it to my mother to cook. She was so pleased to have meat to cook for her family. Mother removed the excess skin, thoroughly washed the head with water, and then placed it in a huge pot filled with clean water. She placed the pot in the fireplace to cook. As the water boiled, she skimmed off the foam that rose to the top of the pot. After it cooked for an hour she added carrots, celery, potatoes, and onions. It smelled so good. We rarely had meat to eat and could hardly wait for our dinner to be ready.

While Mother cooked the cow's head, my brother and I went out to the garden by our house. We gathered dandelion leaves for a salad from the garden. When we returned home we added lemon juice and olive oil to the greens. By now, Mother was ready to serve the meat. We were all thankful for such a wonderful feast. It was like an Easter celebration all over again.

SWEET TIMES WITH MY FATHER

When I was a child, sweets were rare. However, the sweetest and most memorable treat of all occurred after dinner when my father would tell us stories around the kitchen table. My brothers and I sat around him on little, rectangular, wooden stools by to the kitchen fireplace. This was a very special event because we often didn't see Father in the evenings.

There were times during the late fall and winter when Father would be gone for days at a time, traveling from village to village to try to trade a goat, or pig, or a lamb for other items we needed. My Father also enjoyed visiting with other men at the kafenio where they would play cards. Sometimes he came home empty-handed after gambling and I would witness my mother's tears. She would be sad and disappointed but kept it to herself. I remember asking my father, "Did you bring us anything, Father?" and he would answer, "Not this time." I was sad to see my mother's tears but I was too young to understand the full impact of what was happening.

Father was a great storyteller and was very expressive. He also had the ability to recite and write poetry. One of the stories I remember our father telling us was of the events of the Trojan War. It fascinated me to hear how clever Ulysses was in defeating the Trojans with his wooden horse. When Father finished his story he would dismiss us to go to bed. We put on our cotton nightgowns and Mother hugged us goodnight. Before going to bed, we would stop in front of the icons of the Virgin Mary and Christ to say our prayers.

Whenever my father was home in the evenings, he took time to help me learn how to read. I was about six years old when I started school. That first year of school was very difficult for me. I was slow to comprehend the first grade reading book. Furthermore, mother was not able to help me, as she could not read or write. However, she had a great memory and learned most of the songs and stories she knew from other people reading them to her. In those days it was not considered important for girls to go to school. Rather, it was more important that they learn how to cook, do hand embroidery, and weave blankets on the loom for their dowry.

Father helped me to learn to read and pronounce words in the book syllable by syllable. Little by little I learned how to read my first grade book. By the end of the school year I received excellent grades. My father was so proud when I became an honor student. To show his appreciation, one Sunday afternoon, after school was over, he decided to build a puppet stage for my brothers and I.

He took apart an old wooden crate and in a few hours he had a stage ready for us.

My friends came over to my house with their mothers to help us make puppets. We designed the puppets on cardboard boxes and then colored the figures with crayons. We cut the arms off and reconnected them to the shoulders with yarn so that they could move up and down. We did the same with the head and legs. We decided that the first show would be *Little Red Riding Hood* and we worked all afternoon making our puppet characters. My Father said he would give the best storyteller a prize of ten drachmas. We thought that was a lot of money, enough to buy three ice cream cones, which we enjoyed in the hot weather. Every weekend that summer we had a story ready for a puppet show. Grownups and children participated in the plays. It was a lot of fun and that was a summer I recall with fond memories.

HOME REMEDIES

I remember one winter night when Uncle Nicholas came for a visit after dinner bringing a bag of chestnuts and some candy. We put the chestnuts in the fireplace and while they were roasting we sat around the fireplace staying warm. Uncle Nicholas took his seat on a bench close to the fireplace, his face glowing from the firelight as he told stories that he made up as he went along.

While we were listening to his stories and warming by the fire, I accidentally knocked over a pot of hot water that my mother was heating to make tea. The hot water scalded my foot. My mother immediately put my foot in a pale of cold water. I was in so much pain that my mother had to sit up with me all night keeping my foot in the cool water. My foot took a month to heal, as I recall, but I was very lucky because it healed without leaving a scar.

Mother's home remedies healed us many times. I remember having many earaches during the winter. Mother would take a clove of garlic, dip it in warm olive oil, and place it in my ear. The clove of garlic had to be large because it would shrink as it got warm and might go into the ear canal. Within three days the earache would be gone.

I remember other remedies from my childhood. For fever, Mother dipped a cloth into cold water mixed with vinegar and placed it on our foreheads. To stop bleeding, she would wrap a bandage above the wound to act as a tourniquet. Then she took some white clay soil, sieved it, heated it in a frying pan, and mixed it with boiling water to make a paste. She would place it right on top of the wound. Boils were treated with onions and olive oil soap. Mother baked the onion until it was soft and then shaved some olive oil soap on top of it. This was applied directly to the boil. Healing occurred within a few days.

There were many remedies for colds. I recall Mother taking a shaft of wheat, heating it in a frying pan, and then placing it in a small satchel. She would then rub our chests with olive oil and place the satchel of warm wheat on top to maintain the warmth. This would break up the phlegm and help get rid the cold. If we were coughing, Mother would make tea from dried sage and honey. We had to have a cup every four hours.

Mother's remedy for a toothache was simple: it consisted of drinking ouzo. Every two hours she would offer a small amount of ouzo that was swished and held in the mouth for a few minutes. I always felt sorry for the men in our family. It seemed like they were always getting a toothache.

A WEDDING

One of the memorable events of my early childhood was the wedding of my father's sister, Aunt Maria, who got married during the summer. This magnificent wedding that I remember so well almost didn't happen. Maria's eager fiancé stole her from her family's house in a nearby village and brought her to my father's house with thoughts of eloping. As soon as my father opened the door and saw his sister with this young man he was very angry and told him, "You go and take her right back home or I'll shoot you!"

The young man heeded my father's warning and said that he would take Maria back that night and promised that they would soon set a date for the wedding. They later decided on an August wedding date. Of course our family was invited. We would need to travel two hours by foot to my grandmother's village, Avdou for the wedding.

The day arrived and my father got the donkey ready. He lifted my younger brother, Eleftherios, who was two years old onto the donkey. The rest of us walked. Mother brought a bottle of water and a brightly colored wool satchel filled with dried figs and almonds to eat along the way. We left early in the morning before the sun rose. As we departed through the town, a rooster crowed and another answered. The birds were flying from branch to branch chirping. The fresh morning air felt good on my face. As we were traveling, Mother said to Father, "Stop by our grape vineyards to fill the basket with grapes for Yiayia." Father picked some grapes for us to eat also. They were so sweet and cool and refreshing from the morning dew.

Finally, we arrived at Yiayia's house. It had been about six months since we saw her last. My Yiayia was a widow and I never knew my grandfather, as he had passed away several years before. It was always a joy to see my yiayia because she received us with such love and warmth. She would always have food prepared in anticipation of our arrival. She came out to welcome us saying, "Come in, I just made a huge bowl of *loukoumades*. Sit down. I'll bring the nuts and the honey. Use as much as you want." The *loukoumades* (dessert made with fried dough) were nice and warm and tasted delicious.

We then rested for a while until Yiayia called to tell us it was time to get ready for the wedding. Mother brought a white dress she had made for me and she gave me a white ribbon to put in my hair. I was so proud of that special dress my mother made for me to attend the wedding. It made me feel like a princess. My brothers dressed in new pants and white shirts. My father also had put on a new pair of black slacks and a white shirt. My mother looked stunning in a light blue silk dress that she had made. This was the first wedding that I had attended so it was a new experience to see all of us dressed in new clothes. Everyone was so happy to be together. When we were all ready, Yiayia and the rest of our family got together to walk to the church as part of a bridal procession.

The custom was for the bride's relatives and guests to meet at her house while the groom's relatives and guests met at the his house. With Maria's family leading the way, we proceeded to the church to unite the couple and their families. When we arrived at the church it was full, as it was customary to invite people from all the surrounding villages. The wedding ceremony lasted about one hour. My aunt Maria was beautifully dressed in a white wedding gown and the groom had black pants with a white shirt.

After the wedding ceremony, musicians playing the violin, *bouzouki*, and Cretan *lyra* escorted the bride and groom back to the bride's house with the guests and relatives following behind. The house was a gift from my grandfather who was a stonemason and had built the house for my aunt as a wedding gift. It was two stories with two bedrooms upstairs, a family room downstairs, a dining room, and a small kitchen. Young girls would collect items they had sewn throughout there adolescence. These items became part of the girl's dowry. Yiayia stretched ropes in the house and hung my aunt's dowry handiwork. Displayed were crocheted tablecloths, loom-made red blankets decorated on the edge with a row of hand embroidered flowers, and pink and green doilies. They were amazing works of art.

The reception was in the backyard of the home. The men were roasting lambs in the backyard, drinking ouzo and having a great time. Once in a while, someone from the family would call the couple to have a drink together and wish them many years of happiness. The women cooked a variety of dishes in their homes and brought them to the bride's house. They set a table in the backyard in a buffet style and invited the guests to help themselves. People ate and drank for hours and then began singing rhymes for the bride. My father sang songs for the bride and groom. People sang and danced until midnight. We slept at Yiayias' that night. This was the first wedding I can remember and the memories have stayed with me through the years.

THE GRAPE HARVEST

My parents had small parcels of land scattered in different parts of the hills around Mohos. On some parcels they planted grape vineyards and on other parcels they planted olive trees. Still other areas were planted with fruit trees such as apricot, peach, cherry, apple, pear and fig. Figs were a very important fruit that my parents planted. They were dried and sold to the dealers in the city of Iraklion to be exported.

My parents grew Thompson Seedless grapes to be turned into raisins. These white grapes are larger than the grapes used for currants. I remember that whenever currants were mentioned my father would tell us that currants thrive in Corinth and in the Peloponesos, where the land is fertile. He said that the English word currant come from the name Corinth.

Most people cultivated their grapes carefully, digging small ditches around each vine in order to collect the rainwater. To protect against pests the leaves were sprayed with copper sulfate in the early spring. We all prayed for a good harvest.

A few weeks after my aunt's wedding, it was time to harvest the grapes. My parents worked in the vineyards all day long, cutting the grapes and then hanging them on trellises to dry. They would dry in four or five days depending on how hot the weather was.

Harvesting grapes was a lot of fun. We harvested red and green grapes from the vineyards in August and September. My father would place two long round willow baskets on either side of our donkey. These would be used to hold the grapes we collected. We would leave early in the morning before the sun rose and not return until the hot summer sun descended below the small distant hills. Some people were fortunate enough to have broad brimmed straw hats to wear as protection from the sun. At noon we would rest in our bamboo shacks on beds and seats made of compacted sagebrush. We brought enough food from home to last us the day. Mother gave us bread, olives, stewed vegetables, and stuffed zucchini for lunch that day.

The older boys and girls helped their parents cut grapes from the vines with a special hooked knife after which they placed them in the large willow baskets. My job was to carry metal buckets filled with grapes and empty them into the baskets, then take the bucket back to be filled with grapes again. When the baskets on the donkey were filled with grapes they would be taken to the village.

Nearly every household had a large square cement vat to place grapes into. Boys, girls, and adults would wash their feet in order to press the grapes by stomping or dancing up and down in the vat. There would be a wooden barrel positioned at a spout built into the vat to collect the grape juice that would become wine. It could take the whole day to do this depending on how many grapes there were to crush. This entire process would take several days because the grapes ripened at different times.

At the end of each grape-crushing season we had a party. My mother would roast *loukaniko* (pork sausage) over hot coals and made some warm some bread to go with it. We would also have a big tomato and cucumber salad, fresh watermelon with cantaloupe, and fresh succulent figs. Uncle Nicholas would get his *lyra* and suggest that we have a jig or sing some *madinades*. These are songs that are made up spontaneously while singing. Each ending phrase has to rhyme with the previous one. The lyrics speak of the singer's life, family, and friends. Many times the words express the singer's accomplishments in their work or they joke about some blunder that occurred, causing everyone to burst out laughing. From beginning to end, no matter how hard the work, the grape harvesting and crushing time in Mohos was always enjoyable.

THE FEAST DAY OF THE FALLING ASLEEP OF THE VIRGIN MARY

August fifteenth is the feast of the Falling Asleep of the Virgin Mary in the Orthodox Church, which is a big feast day. Thousands of people would come from the villages surrounding Mohos to celebrate the feast day of the Virgin Mary at our church, which was named in her honor. Some even came from the city of Iraklion to celebrate with us. Our church of the Panagia was built in the Byzantine style and was located on the southern side of the main square in Mohos.

Since the Falling Asleep is such a large feast day, there are many preparations that take place. The restaurant owners would prepare their restaurants with great detail, working for weeks before the event. They would whitewash the fronts of their buildings and bring geranium plants from their homes to place by the doors of their restaurants. They washed the sidewalks and put new tablecloths on the tables. Eventually, they would string colorful flags from branch to branch on the mulberry trees surrounding the plateia.

The ladies would bake round loaves of sweet bread called, *artos*, which they took to church before the Divine Liturgy began. These loaves represent the five loaves of bread and two fish that the Bible tells us Jesus blessed and then used to feed a crowd of five thousand people. Each family brings five loaves along with a list of the names of their family members written on a piece of paper. The lists are given to the parish priest so that he can pray for each person by name when he blesses the *artos*. Some churches received fifty loaves or more.

The women would also be busy preparing other delicacies such as *baklava*, *kourambiedes*, and *diples*. These are are thin strips of dough, about three inches wide, that are fried and rolled and then topped with hot honey syrup and sprinkled with nuts and cinnamon.

Early on the morning of the fifteenth (the day of the feast) families go to church to pray and listen to the priest tell the story of the significance of the death of the Virgin Mary. When the Liturgy is over, the priest blesses the loaves of bread and chants a traditional hymn:

> *Rich men have turned poor and gone hungry, but those who seek the Lord shall never be deprived of any good thing.*

Each person then receives a piece of the sweet *artos*

bread as they exit the church into the platia, which already smells of lamb and sausage roasting. Men with the musical instruments would begin to play their music and after we had eaten the men and women in their traditional costumes begin to dance. In traditional Cretan dances the best male dancer leads a circle of dancers and does all the tricky steps.

My yiayia told me, "Hundreds of years ago, before we became more civilized, only men were allowed to dance." Today everyone enjoys dancing, men, women, and children together. Music, dancing, and feasting continue well past midnight. Everyone enjoys visiting with each other, catching up on the news from each other's villages, and telling stories and making jokes. Good wishes are exchanged among relatives and friends for a happy and healthy life until next year's festival.

SNAILS AND SPOOKS

During the summer, snails conceal themselves in the cavities of trees (particularly olive trees), which makes it difficult to find them. However, when the first rains come in autumn, snails begin to come out in droves. Men, women, and children would take oil lamps and baskets into the orchards to collect the huge snails at night. One could see the light of oil lamps for miles around, appearing like lightening bugs in the distance.

I remember while gathering snails one year, we heard a strange roar coming from a nearby cemetery. We children had often heard the adults speaking amongst themselves, saying that many people had heard strange noises coming from the cemetery at night. It was rumored that a ghost lived there. Now, we all heard the noise. The closer we got to the cemetery, the louder the roar became. My father, being a brave man, said to us, "Stay with your mother while I go inside the cemetery to see what is making that roar."

My brothers and I were so scared that we hid behind my mother's long skirts. We could not see Father from where we were standing because a six-foot wall surrounded the cemetery. We shook with fright, waiting for my father to come out. The roaring finally stopped but Father still hadn't returned. It took him the longest time to appear. He finally emerged from the cemetery and walked over to us. He had solved the mystery. There was a horse tied to a tree in the cemetery with a rope. When the horse walked around and around the tree, the rope became shorter and shorter causing the horse to choke himself. Father decided to turn the horse loose by cutting the rope from the tree. Now we could continue to collect the huge snails until our baskets were almost full.

We carried our baskets home and mother fed the live snails wheat chaff until they were saturated. She let the snails sit for several days to purify themselves before she cooked them. Escargot provided good protein for us when we could not afford to buy meat. There were many different ways to cook the snails but my favorite way was to bake them in their shells with garlic and butter. They were so delicious.

The day after our snail gathering, Father heard that the horse had returned to his home but had cuts on his neck caused by pulling on the rope. A few days later Father saw the owner and told him what had happened. The owner thanked him for saving the horse's life. From then on, Father liked to tell the story about the cemetery having a ghost- and the ghost was a horse.

OLIVES IN OCTOBER

Olives were harvested between October and December. Olive trees have been cultivated in Greece since ancient times. Olive trees, with their gnarly trunks and silvery leaves, can live almost anywhere except the mountains. They don't grow very tall but they live for a long time. Some olive trees planted in the thirteenth century are still yielding olives today.

In the early fall, my parents began preparing to harvest our olives. They repaired burlap sacks to hold the olives and sewed others together to make a large burlap blanket, as they would require a huge blanket to go around the bigger olive trees. Later, when they went to harvest the olives, they would stretch the burlap blanket on the ground around the base of the olive tree and then beat the branches with sticks, causing olives to fall down onto the burlap blanket. From there they were scooped into sacks, loaded onto the donkey, and taken to the factory to be pressed into olive oil.

Green olives were harvested in September and

October, while black olives were gathered from November through January. I remember going with my father on cold winter nights to watch men press olives by pushing a grindstone with a heavy log. In those days, the olives that were taken to the factory were pressed by manpower on a grindstone wheel that was about seven feet in diameter. It was very hard work and it took three men to push the wheel over the olives. This was such a strenuous job that they changed men every hour. My father worked in the village factory pressing olives for the entire pressing season. While Father worked there he made sure we got the first press from our olives, as the first press yields the finest olive oil.

The process for the second pressing of olives is very different than the process for the first. The remains of the olive skins from the first pressing, along with the pits, are heated at a high temperature in order to extract more oil. This results in a stronger acidity and makes the olive oil taste a little sharp. The acidity of the processed olive oil is measured by degrees in the factory. If it is too sharp, the merchants mix in other oils to reduce the sharp taste.

When a person goes to the store to purchase a bottle of olive oil labeled *Extra Virgin Olive Oil*, it does not mean that they really get quality olive oil. The reason for this is that the merchant mixes all kinds of oil together to fill the barrels. Naturally, they label this *Extra Virgin* as long as it comes from olives but the quality is not there. It is widely believed that some of the best olives in the world come from Greece. It takes four to five liters of olives to make one liter of olive oil. If a person is very lucky they will be there to taste the very first cold press that comes through the spout. You would never forget the delicious flavor of freshly pressed virgin olive oil and mashed garlic on fresh, home baked bread.

The olive trees continued to provide for us, even after the olives were harvested. Sheets of crushed olive pits about one inch thick were left behind when the pressing was done. The workers stack these pit sheets one on top of the other and carry them home to dry and use as firewood.

When the pressing of our olives was completed it was time to prune the olive trees. My father pruned all our trees and cut the branches into smaller pieces to bundle up and load onto the donkey. This olive wood was carried home to Mother to use for cooking and to warm our house during the winter. Growing up, the olive tree was truly our tree of life.

CELEBRATING CHRISTMAS AND THE NEW YEAR

A few days before Christmas, my brothers and I, along with the neighborhood children, would go from house to house singing Christmas carols. We carried baskets that the women of the houses we visited would fill with cookies, raisins, and nuts. On Christmas Day, Mother filled plates with pastries and cookies for my brothers and I to take to various friends and relatives. In turn, they would give us plates with sweets so that we had various pastries and cookies to last for weeks. Besides this holiday, it was always a rare occasion when we had sweets. It was only during the major feast days, perhaps three times a year, that it was a tradition to make sweets for the family. The rest of the year we had fresh fruit, nuts, or raisins for dessert.

This Christmas in December 1931, my parents decided we would go to Yiayia's village to celebrate. Mother had just given birth to twin boys in the first week of November and Yiayia had not seen them yet. Mother thought it would be joyful for all of us to celebrate Christmas together at Yiayia's. On Christmas Eve I was so excited. I got up early in the morning and to helped Mother pack a huge basket for Yiayia. It was filled with cookies and Christmas bread, Yiayia's favorite.

Father borrowed a horse from the neighbors so that Mother could ride while holding the twins. My brothers rode on the donkey while my father and I walked. It was about two hours walking up a rocky trail. We sang Christmas carols as we walked, making the distance feel shorter. When we arrived at the top of the hill we could see the valley below, as well as the first snowfall across Dikti Mountain. Along the southern side of this mountain is the entrance to a deep cave known as the Diktaion Antron where, according to legend, Zeus was born. On top of the mountain is a plateau called Lassithi that is the best agricultural area in the region due to an abundance of water windmills.

We finally reached Yiayia's village. Sometimes, during January, snow covers the entire village for a couple of days, giving children the opportunity to have fun playing in a winter wonderland. As we came closer to Yiayia's house, we smelled the aroma of freshly baked bread coming from the village ovens. Yiayia was waiting at the door. She welcomed us with great joy, hugging us as tears of joy streamed down her cheeks. She kissed all of us and then took the twins in her arms. She admired them and didn't want to set them down. However, one of the neighbors brought in a cradle and she put them down to sleep.

Since we were still fasting in preparation for Christmas, Yiayia made lentil soup served with olives and homemade whole-wheat bread. After we finished lunch Yiayia asked my father to butcher her pig, as it was customary to have roast pig for Christmas. On Christmas morning Father helped Yiayia light an outdoor oven to roast a portion of the pig. Other families also brought their own meat for Christmas dinner to roast in Yiayia's oven and Yiayia shared some of her meat with families that did not have a pig to slaughter. Any remaining meat was boiled and then stored in ceramic crock-pots. The cooked fat from the pig was poured on top to keep it from spoiling.

My father's two younger sisters (who lived with Yiayia) helped peel potatoes to roast with the meat and Mother made salad. My Aunt Maria and her husband came to celebrate Christmas with us too. The smell of roast pork tantalized us all morning and we were all so happy to sit down together to share this most special day.

New Year's Eve was also a special celebration. The day before New Year, my mother would make the traditional Vasilopita bread. The name Vasilopita is derived from Saint. Basil the Great was an early Church Father from Caesarea in Cappadocia. The Orthodox Church celebrates his name day on New Year's Day. Legend says that he gave coins to children on New Year's Day, therefore, the Orthodox faithfully carry out a tradition of placing a coin into the dough of the Vasilopita before it is baked.

On New Year's Eve Mother would invite friends

and relatives to our house to celebrate the coming year. Around nine at night, everybody gathered around the table to play card games. Mother made *loukoumades* to pass around while we sang about Saint Basil coming from Caesarea to bring us gifts. Around midnight, when the church bells rang out, we turned off our oil and kerosene lamps and sang an old song that speaks of the old year having gone and our hope that the new one would bring happiness and joy. We lit the lamps again and Mother cut the sweet Vasilopita bread. All the children impatiently gathered around the table to see who would get the coin in their piece of bread. According to custom, whoever finds the coin in their slice of Vasilopita is sure to have a very lucky year.

The next day, New Year's Day, we would usually go to church services and then have lunch with our family. After lunch, our aunts and uncles would bring each child a small basket filled with candy and cookies along with a few coins placed in the bottom of the basket. This was both our Christmas and New Year's gift, a perfect ending to our holidays.

CHOLERA

A great epidemic of cholera broke out in the village of Mohos in February of 1931. People were dying every day. I recall looking out the windows of my house and seeing funeral processions going by in the distance. I could hear the mourners crying out loud for their loved ones. It broke my heart to hear their wails. It was frightening to see so many people dying because there was no cure.

I remember seeing the concern on my parents' faces as they wondered if it be one of us next. The doctor told Mother that the only thing she could do was to keep us in the house, away from sick people, and to make sure all our drinking water was boiled. This disease plagued the village for most of that winter. It was very frightening to not know who would be the next to contract cholera.

It was very cold that winter, snowing twice in one month. Since there was no central heat in the house, water froze in the jugs. No matter how much wood Mother put in the fireplace we could not get warm. It was the end of February when my twin baby brothers became sick with colds that turned into pneumonia. Mother called the doctor whose only suggestion was to keep them warm and to apply warm cloths to their chests. Mother tried everything she could to help the babies break up the phlegm in their chests but within a few days, they took a turn for the worse. They coughed and coughed but nothing came up. Mother was scared and went to get the priest to baptize them.

Father arranged for the godparents to meet us at church. The priest performed an emergency baptism. Mother named the babies Michael and George in honor of her brothers. One week later my twin brothers died. They were three months old. Uncle Nicholas built a small wooden coffin and painted it light blue. He drew a golden angel on each side. Mother dressed the twins in their white baptism clothes and placed them in the coffin. She draped a beautiful floral blanket she had made by hand over the coffin.

Our neighbors and relatives came and mourned the loss of the babies with Mother. We children gathered around the tiny coffin and cried at the loss of our brothers. It was the saddest day for all of us. The priest led a procession to the cemetery for the burial. After the funeral service, we all returned home where my aunt, Kaliope, had prepared shrimp and rice for all the people. Mother mourned the twins every day. She went to the cemetery at least once a week and bent over the gravesite, crying her heart out. My brothers and I went along and cried with her.

MY GRANDFATHER'S STORY

It was 1911 when my grandfather left Greece and traveled to America. He left behind his wife, my father, Manoli, who was then eight years old, and a daughter, Maria, six years old. When World War One broke out in July of 1914, traveling from America to other countries was difficult. Therefore, Grandfather did not return to Greece until 1918 when the war was over.

When Grandfather returned from America to Avdou, his village in Crete, the whole town welcomed him with great celebration. The town hall and the school were decorated with Greek flags and the church bells rang loudly to proclaim to everyone that Michael Vasiloyianakis had returned from America, the victorious country that had liberated the entire world. It was a great celebration. Girls danced in colorful costumes, men roasted lamb in a big barbecue pit, and everyone rejoiced. My grandmother remembered the occasion well and told me stories about the speech Grandfather gave. He told everyone about the greatness of America and that if a person worked hard in America they had opportunity to become successful. My grandmother recalled that everyone cheered, clapped, and wished for America to live forever.

My Grandfather settled in Avdou and worked very hard to make a good living for his family. He grew vineyards and specialized in making wine for commercial markets. As his vineyards grew so did his family. A year after his return to Crete, my grandmother gave birth to a third child, Polymia. Two years later another baby was born. She was the third daughter and was baptized Athena. My father, Manoli, was the only surviving son and was twenty years older than his youngest sister. Grandfather's firstborn son died tragically when he was ten years old. He was running and fell into an open well that was uncovered and drowned before he could be rescued.

Tragedy struck again in 1928 when my grandfather became ill with tuberculosis. There were no antibiotics in those days and doctors sent stricken patients to a special hospital called a sanatorium. Grandfather was ordered to go to a sanatorium that was located on the outskirts of the city of Iraklion. After several months he felt better and grandmother asked if she could bring him home. The doctor said yes but only if he was isolated from the people in the village. He explained that tuberculosis was an infectious disease that could be spread very rapidly as a result of close contact with an infected person.

Grandmother decided to take Grandfather five miles away from the village, to a church called Saint Photini that sat on a hill. Near the church was a cave used by the Orthodox priests during the Turkish Occupation of Greece. During the occupation it was forbidden to teach Christianity, so the priests risked their own lives by gathering the children in this cave at night to provide them with *Cathiyitiko* (Sunday School). When the weather was mild the children would assemble at the foot of the hill and climb in procession to the cave at the top, guided by the light of the moon. During the winter there was no *Cathiyitiko,* as there was snow on the hill, making the path icy, slippery, and dangerous for nighttime travel. The priests held fast to the Greek culture and Christian religion by teaching the children during those dark years from 1460 to1821 CE. The Greek nation endured the tyranny of the Ottoman Empire for almost four hundred years and yet the priests continued to secretly educate the children this entire time. There is a famous song commemorating the joy of the children on their nighttime journey up the hillside to the cave beside Saint Photini. Every Greek schoolchild learns this song. I remember singing it when I was a child.

The first few words are, "Little moon, light my way…"

It was here in this very cave, years later, that my grandfather lived, sick and isolated from his family and village. He endured this lonely existence for two years. Every day my grandmother cooked food at home and walked the five miles to the cave to bring him sustenance. Once a week the village priest would travel to Saint Photini Church by donkey to perform the Divine Liturgy. He made weekly visits to my grandfather. As time went on, Grandfather became weaker and weaker until he finally passed away. He was fifty-five years old.

MY YIAYIA

After my grandfather became sick with tuberculosis and died, Yiayia had to work in order to support herself and her two young daughters, Polymia and Athena. Grandmother was a hard worker and a very energetic lady. She was extremely talented and knowledgeable in a variety of handcrafts. She could weave beautiful baskets, rope for chair cushions, and sandals for young girls. However, her specialty was in designing and weaving patterns for the loom. Grandmother owned her own loom and taught her daughters to make their own blankets, bed sheets, and pillowcases in addition to many other articles for home use.

Almost every household in the village had a loom but most of the women did not have the skill to thread the loom or set the design they desired. Yiayia was expert in this intricate work and was hired by other women who required a pattern to be set or a loom to be threaded. Grandmother also taught young girls how to spin wool into yarn.

After a sheep is sheared, the wool has to be washed and dried before it can be spun into yarn. Yiayia would dye the wool various colors according to the designed pattern. She often invented designs of her own to be woven into the fabric. I still have some of the articles she designed in 1920. The fabric remains strong and the colors vibrant.

Grandmother was a strong woman. Besides loosing her son and husband at young ages, from time to time she also cared for orphans whose parents died had from cholera or other diseases. I remember playing with these orphans when I was a child. Grandmother said that people who take the time to help the unfortunate will be marked in the Book of Life in Heaven and God will make angels of them. I admire my Yiayia for her many talents, but most of all, I admire her for her wisdom, moral character, and guidance to my as a child. She taught me how to live a virtuous and righteous life. She taught us with her words and showed us with her deeds.

My Yiayia unwinding thread a spindle. She was an expert at setting looms.

Samples of My Grandmother's Weaving, Embroidery and Crochet Work

MY FATHER'S MEMORIES OF THE TURKISH-GREEK CONFLICT (1919-1923)

"An armistice was signed at Moudania, in Anatolia, on October 11, 1922. A conference of all the powers interested in restoring peace to the Near East met in Lausanne in January 1923. The Turkish-Greek accord that resulted on 30 January provided for the repatriation of all civilian internees on both sides regardless of number, as well all of the Turkish prisoners of war and an equal number of Greek prisoners of war. The remainder of the Greek prisoners of war was to be repatriated after signing the peace treaty, which took place on 24 July 1923." - International Committee of the Red Cross

War broke out between Turkey and Greece in 1921 and lasted for three years. As a young man, my father was drafted to fight the Turks on the front line. He was captured soon after being drafted and was in prison for ten months. After my father returned home, he would talk to his father about the conditions while he was a prisoner of war. He related that the prisoners were clothed only in burlap sacks and were forced to stand shivering in the cold for over four hours at a time. They suffered in a crowded disease-ridden prison that carried the stench of urine and excrement. It was impossible to keep clean for lack of running water.

When I was growing up my Yiayia recounted the stories that my father had told Grandfather before I was born. My father had told about meals that were served three times a day and consisted of the same thing every time – boiled water with either macaroni or rice along with iron hard stale bread. He talked about the frequent incidences of malnutrition and rampant tuberculosis. "Water was scarce," my father told Grandfather. "Because we were not allowed to wash, skin infections broke out all over our sweaty, dirty bodies. Many of the prisoners suffered from toothaches. I had several rotting teeth, which gave me a very bad headache. I could not stand the pain any longer and then one day, a prisoner who had dental training ordered two other prisoners to hold me down while he extracted my teeth with pliers. I was in great pain for weeks and had no medication to relieve the pain.

We prisoners always had to be on the alert for unexpected inspections. Guards with fixed bayonets would suddenly rush in at any time of the day or night. They were suspicious of prisoners trying to escape by stealing guns or overtaking the night guards who were not minding their jobs. We had to stand in absolute silence. After those ten months in prison the war was over. I lost fifty pounds and my hair was full of lice. My stomach could not hold any food because my digestive system was too weak. Anything I ate or drank caused nausea and vomiting. I had severe abdominal pain and cramping, followed by diarrhea. This occurred about every twenty minutes.

After the war was over, the Turkish government allowed all the prisoners to be released. Finally, I had permission to return home. I was lonely and desperate to see my family and so I took the first boat available and returned to Crete. When the boat landed in the harbor I stepped out and kissed the soil, thankful that God spared my life and allowed me to see the island of Crete once again."

Father told about taking a bus to his village, about thirty-five kilometers from the city of Iraklion. "The roads were not paved; many curves and huge holes made the trip difficult for both the driver and passengers. The driver had to stop often, as many people became sick and had to vomit. The trip took almost two hours."

When he finally arrived, his mother, father, and three sisters were there to welcome him, along with the entire village. "They all gathered to celebrate my arrival. I was a hero to them but I was too sick to enjoy their enthusiasm. I needed to go home."

Yiayia told us that my father remembered every detail of his homecoming and would often relate details to friends and family. "My mother told my oldest sister, Maria, to light the fire and heat some water for a bath. It was December and I was shivering. We had no bathroom so I washed at the tap the best I could. After I bathed, my mother gave me my father's clean pants and shirt to wear. In the meantime, she burned all the clothes I wore home, afraid that they were full of lice. Then my father shaved all the hair off my head. Mother asked one of the villagers to get the doctor in order to examine me. When the doctor arrived, I was shaved and clean but very weak from malnutrition. The doctor ordered medication to reduce the vomiting and told me to start my diet by drinking liquids like chicken broth and taking frequent sips of hot tea. The next day, I could try to eat a soft boiled egg with toasted bread."

"I will return in a few days to see how you are doing," said the doctor. "In the meantime, get all the rest you can." With the doctor's advice and the loving care of his family, my father grew stronger each day. He gained weight and his cheeks became rosy. Yiayia remembered that it took a whole year for him to feel like himself again.

Two years later, my father met my mother at a wedding. Six months after they first met, he asked her father's blessing for his daughter's hand in marriage. They had a big wedding celebration that lasted almost a week. Friends and relatives came from surrounding villages, either by foot or by donkey. My father could now look ahead to his life.

A MEMORABLE FIRST GRADE

I entered first grade in the fall of 1931. My school was near the Panagia Church beside the plateia. The school building was built out of stone, which was covered with white stucco. A red-tiled roof and red window shutters gave it a colorful appearance. The six rooms were big enough to accommodate the first through sixth grades. The schoolyard was surrounded by pomegranate, apple, and fig trees. When the fruit was ripe, students had free fruit for lunch. The school playground was large enough for us to do our daily gymnastics or to play various games like hopscotch, catch-the-wolf, and jump rope.

Hygiene, manners, and discipline were all part of our education. Every day, before entering the classroom, students formed lines for hygiene inspection. Our fingernails needed to be trimmed and our hands clean. There was a faucet in the playground for students that did not pass inspection to wash. If we were late for school we received three strokes across the palm with a switch. We were not likely to forget this severe punishment. Our palms stung for quite some time. When the teacher entered the classroom students stood at attention and the room fell silent. It was only after being given permission that we were allowed to sit down. If we didn't turn in our homework on time the teacher would make us write out our spelling words ten times each. If we misbehaved the teacher would send a note home to our parents. When this happened to me my father spanked me with a switch. I remember feeling like my behind was on fire. Father did not spank me often but when he did I remembered it for a very long time. Discipline was always strictly enforced and taken seriously. After all the spankings and discipline I received from my teacher and my father, I always understood what I did wrong and I respected them for correcting me so that I would not do the same thing again.

My teacher, Mrs. Eleni, taught first and second grade in the same room. She provided instruction in the alphabet, reading, writing, music, and Greek folk dance. She taught the girls cross-stitch embroidery and taught the boys how to build model houses and boats from cardboard boxes. She taught music to everyone and assigned children's songs to each grade. Once we memorized the songs, the entire class sang together. It was enchanting to hear all those voices blending into one. I enjoyed singing in class twice a week and it gave me confidence to learn even more songs.

My father spent evenings reviewing my school lessons and helping me learn how to read and write. Learning was difficult for me but he had a great deal of patience. By the end of the school year, with his help, I finished the first grade with strait A's. While my father taught me academics, my mother taught me handicrafts. It was during this first year at school that my mother taught my girlfriends, Antonia, and Georgia, and I how to knit and crochet. By the time New Year's arrived, we all knew how to knit and each of us completed a pair of slippers for our mothers.

In the last two months before school was out, Mrs. Eleni assigned songs or poems to children who wished to participate in a commencement ceremony at the end of the school year. Mrs. Eleni said, "Since Aristea has a good and loud voice, I am assigning her to sing the national anthem at the opening ceremony." I was surprised to be selected to sing the national anthem and I felt great pride and honor to be the one student chosen to begin the ceremony and to sing about the country I loved.

We worked for many hours the week before the opening ceremony. The auditorium room was large enough to accommodate two hundred people. There was a stage at one end, which we decorated with a string of small Greek flags. On each side of the stage we placed huge pots filled with bay leaf branches and on each branch we tied blue and white balloons that floated upward, restricted by the string. All the girls' embroidery was arranged on the walls of the auditorium. On the right side of the room, on big long tables, the boys displayed their model homes and boats.

The day of the commencement ceremonies finally arrived. I was very nervous and excited at the same time. The parents were allowed to enter the auditorium one hour before the ceremony began to inspect and admire our artwork. In a short time, the auditorium was packed to the point that many people had to stand in the side aisles. The school principal introduced our teacher, Mrs. Eleni, and said what a splendid job she had done in teaching the children. Mrs. Eleni thanked him and everybody gave her a standing ovation. Mrs. Eleni then began the program by saying, "The children have rehearsed for many weeks. Please take your seats and enjoy their performance. Aristea will open the ceremony by singing the national anthem."

I got up on the stage and looked out at the people. There was not a sound in the room. For a long moment I stood frozen. My heart was beating fast and my knees trembled. People stared at me and began to whisper; I could sense their uneasiness. Suddenly I realized that I could not let my teacher or my parents down. Finally, I swallowed hard, bowed to everyone and began to sing the national anthem as loudly and as proudly as I could.

After I finished, everyone clapped and my teacher gave me a big hug. My parents hugged me too and said how proud they were of me and told me that I did a marvelous job. This was a night I would always remember.

MOVING TO THE CITY

I remember when my father decided he would rather live in the city than in the village. He tried to convince my mother to sell our village property and move. "Why do you think that we will do better by moving to the city?" she asked.

My father then uttered the words that he knew would change my mother's mind. "It will be a better life for our children. They will get a better education in the city." Mother looked at Father with tears in her eyes, not knowing what the future would bring. Although she was afraid, she wanted to do what was best for her children. Father reassured her that he planned to do business in wholesale produce trading with retail stores. He planned to go to the city to look for a house before making the big move. It was decided that we would move at the end of May, after the school year was complete.

Father found a house near Iraklion, a busy port city on the northern coast of Crete. It was in a suburb area called *Hrisopigi* (Golden Fountain). He put a down payment on the house with the understanding that he would pay the remainder in cash when he sold our property in the village. Little by little he sold off our property and paid for the house and still had money left over to start a business.

On the day we moved, Uncle Nicholas helped us load a few bundles of our belongings onto the donkey. Neighbors and friends gathered around to say goodbye and to wish us good luck. We embraced each other with tears in our eyes. I still remember this emotional farewell. The last goodbyes were said and Uncle Nicholas led us to the plaza where a bus was waiting to take us to the city. He waited and waved goodbye until we were boarded. My brothers and I were merrily waving back and I noticed my mother was also waving to Uncle Nicholas, her brother, but she had tears in her eyes.

We arrived at our new house at about three in the afternoon. When I first saw the front of the house, I could not believe that we were actually going to live here. It looked like a mansion compared to our house in the village. The outside walls were painted white and the trim and shutters were green, giving it an appearance as fresh as new grown mint. The front yard was surrounded by a white picket fence that was draped with sweet smelling honeysuckle. It seemed like our new life would be wonderful. We were all very hot and exhausted from our trip and the excitement of moving day. Mother fed us some fruit and bread and we all fell asleep on the floor. Our household goods would soon be delivered by a horse wagon that my father had hired.

Father woke up early the next morning and went into town to buy some furniture. He purchased two double beds and a sofa. One bed was for my parents and the other one was for my brothers to share. Since I was the only girl, I would sleep on the sofa. I recall the headboards of the new beds were all brass, shiny and beautiful. I envied my brothers sleeping in their shiny bed while I slept on the sofa.

I explored our new house and thought it was very pretty. I could see that our house was in a nice neighborhood with a few stores nearby. One was a general store that sold yardage material, crochet yarns, and embroidery thread of all kinds. Upstairs were two large bedrooms with a door that opened onto a balcony. I remember the amazing view of the city from our balcony. At night we could look and see Iraklion covered with electric lights sparkling like thousands of flickering candles. For the first time in my life I saw streetlights and neon signs of various colors that blinked over storefronts.

There was so much to see in the city. I could not believe how different it was compared to our village. Most of the main streets were covered with asphalt. Sidewalks were cemented. Part of the Old City had narrow streets made of cobblestones. Neat small homes with red-tiled roofs lined both sides of the street and geraniums and basil decorated verandas. I was amazed to see that all the homes had running water and electric lights. Some of the wealthier homes even had steam heat. The ones that faced the sea had beautiful gardens and wrought iron fences covered with climbing jasmine. They had a beautiful view of the Mediterranean Sea. Even the store windows amazed me. In the window displays, life-sized mannequins wore the newest styles. They were dressed in suits from England and France for both men and women. At first I thought they were real people. My father told me they were just big dolls standing there to show us the latest clothing styles.

We quickly settled into our new home and became well acquainted with our new city. Located along the northern coast of Crete, Iraklion is one of the chief cities of the island. The population at that time was about forty-five thousand. One of the interesting places was the harbor, which had shipping and trading going on every day. Passenger ships took the twelve-hour rides from Pireaus, near Athens on the mainland, to Iraklion daily.

The Venetian harbor in Iraklion was the most popular seaside area in the city. When the sun goes down in the evening people like to promenade at this harbor. It is about one mile long. At the end of the pier is an old circular tower from which an excellent panoramic view of the ocean and coastline can be seen. After World War Two this tower was transformed into a restaurant. Pedestrians like to rest there while ordering the most delicious barbequed lamb and fish caught that day.

On the east side of Iraklion is a beautiful garden maintained by city workers. The garden is terraced into varying designs like stars, squares, and circles. Each terrace is planted with flowers according to the season. At the middle of the garden is a statue of the Unknown Soldier.

The garden has walking paths that are furnished with benches for pedestrians to rest on. On the west side of the garden, the city built a bandstand to be used by musicians. Most Sunday afternoons find people sitting across the street from the gardens in the plateia, which is surrounded with restaurants and pastry shops. Tables are set on the sidewalk where people can sit, eat dinner, or drink refreshments while listening to the music. This area of town is knows as *Tris Kamares* (Three Arches) even though there are no arches present. The plateia is surrounded with wide avenues that stretch in all directions and are lined with large trees. During the summer, at seven in the evening, the whole city comes alive. Rich and poor put on their best clothes and join each other, promenading back and forth on the main street. I remember joining the crowds with my family. It was as if we were part of a formal procession for the next three hours, often stopping to visiting with each other. We were proud to be part of this beautiful and friendly big city.

Historic sites abound in Iraklion. In the center of the city is another plaza called *Maydonie*, where there is a large forth century fountain decorated with six Venetian lion statues. When the fountain is on, water comes out of the lion's mouths. One of the oldest churches is *Agios Titus* (Saint Titus). This is where Saint Titus' relics were returned to from Saint Mark Basilica of Venice. Agios Titus was one of the apostles of Saint Paul. He was sent to Crete to spread Christ's teachings where he converted many people to Christianity and became the island's first bishop. He lived to be over ninety years old.

Six kilometers south of Iraklion there is a silver-green landscape covered in olive and cypress trees. This is where the palace of the city of Knossos stands. It dates back thousands of years to the time of King Minos. The palace corridors and frescoes are of unmatched beauty and show a high level of culture and civilization. It was a pleasure to take Sunday walks with my friends to the Palace of Knossos. Knossos is imprinted in my mind from all the years I lived in Iraklion. I often wonder how ingenious this Minoan civilization was to build remarkable palaces that have continued to survive for thousands of years. Every year the sight and history of the Minoan palace attracts thousands of visitors from all over the world. I was privileged to grow up near the site of this world treasure.

My Brother Elefterios by the Venetian Fountain in Iraklion in the late 1960s. The city still is a combination of Ancient and Modern.

MY FATHER'S NEW VENTURE

When my father first decided to begin a small produce business, he went to Iraklion to look for a place suitable to use as a warehouse. After searching for a week, he found an ideal two-story building on the outskirts of the city. He could store crates of fruits and vegetables in a cool spot on the first floor. In the front of the building was a large room facing the street that could be turned into a small grocery store. Father approached the owner of the building and came to an agreement for a one-year lease. Father then went to the farmers in the village and signed contracts with them to buy their produce. He made arrangements to take orders a week in advance, as produce had to be used up weekly do to lack of refrigeration. During the summer months, Father had to order blocks of ice to keep the fruit from spoiling.

In order to maximize profits in my father's new business, it was very important to sort out the fruits and vegetables so that the best price could be charged for quality produce. Therefore, my parents arose at seven every morning to walk three miles to the warehouse where they sorted produce. They put perfect, undamaged fruit in one crate to be sold at the wholesale market. The ones with slight damage were put in another crate to be sold in the grocery store at a reduced price. On Saturdays my brothers and I would go along with Mother to help sort out the produce. My father's business grew during the summer months when produce was plentiful. As soon as school was out for the summer we helped sort produce every day. Since I was the oldest child I was also given the task of minding the grocery store while my parents sorted fruit. If I needed help with the customers I would call for my father. Once the produce was sorted, it had to be delivered to retailers twice a week. My parents loaded the truck early in the morning on Wednesdays and Fridays. By eight in the morning they made rounds from store to store and delivered all the orders.

We were closed on Sunday. It was a day of rest. We would often go to church in the morning and then come home for lunch. As soon as lunch was finished we would head to the beach for a fun and restful afternoon. We didn't have far to go, as the sea was only one mile from our house. Mother would pack some snacks and off we would go. I remember going to the beach on a sunny afternoon early in May. My brothers were so excited to see the water that they jumped into the sea wearing their shorts. The water was frigid and they quickly came out shivering. Mother said, "Boys, it is not yet summer! Wait until June or July when the water will be so warm that it will be like taking a bath." We had a wonderful day relaxing together at the beach. The day was clear and the sky so blue. The sun warmed our backs, making us feel good outside and inside. After we rested a while we decided to pick some of the early spring flowers that were growing among the rocks. Mother helped us make wreaths to hang on the door to dry in time for the celebration of May Day and to remind us of our wonderful day by the sea

MOTHER'S MEMORABLE NAME DAY

I remember a particular Sunday afternoon when I was seven years old. After church my family stopped at the kafenio to have *souvlak*i (shish kabob) and french fries. While we were enjoying lunch, a man and woman asked my parents if they could sit at our table, as all the other tables were occupied. They introduced themselves as Olga and Andreas and they were obviously not from Greece. Father asked Andreas where they were from and discovered that they were from Russia and had come to Iraklion as political refugees. They told us about the persecution occurring in Russia since Joseph Stalin had come into power in 1928. Many Orthodox Christians who had been unable to escape to other countries had been put to death. Olga and Andreas were Orthodox Christians, both fifty years old, and had just barely escaped the ruthless executions of Stalin's regime.

Andreas said, "Any Christians who openly expressed their views would be arrested by the communist secret police and either killed outright or else forced into labor in northern Russia or Siberia." During the communist era, many churches were forced to close. Several of them were turned into museums. Despite the persecution, many of the older people kept their faith deep in their hearts and secretly taught the Orthodox religion to their children and grandchildren.

When Andreas finished telling my parents about the sad situation in Russia and about their escape to Greece, Father asked where they were now living. They told him they took shelter in a schoolhouse, sleeping on the cement floor. Andreas wanted to find a proper place to live but he had no money and was unable to find work. My parents felt very sorry for them and offered them our living room until Andreas found some work. Olga and Andreas were so happy that tears came to their eyes. They hugged my mother and father and said that they would never forget their generosity. They moved into our house the next day and became part of our family.

The fifteenth of August, the feast day of the Virgin Mary and my mother's name day, was soon approaching. Mother took me to the fabric store near our neighborhood to buy material for a new dress to wear on the Virgin Mary's feast day. The owner of the shop showed us several fabrics but it was a beautiful white fabric with red polka dots that caught my eye. I looked into my mother's eyes hoping she would say yes to the one I chose. She returned my pleading look with a big smile. She hugged me and said, "I like that one, too." Since mother did not have a sewing machine she gave the material to a seamstress to make the dress for me. When it was finished I put it on and twirled around, looking at myself in the mirror and thinking it was the most beautiful dress I had ever owned. It had ruffled sleeves and ruffles around the neck. I loved my new dress. Mother then bought me new red shoes to match. I was filled with joy.

The feast day of the Virgin Mary arrived and I felt like I was the best-dressed girl in town. All my friends looked at me in admiration. We went to services at a church near the plaza that was called the Virgin Mary, just like our church in Mohos. It was almost like the Virgin Mary had followed us from the village to the city.

Before we left for church that morning my parents prepared a leg of lamb that Father purchased from the butcher shop the previous night. Father prepared potatoes to go with the lamb, while Mother prepared sauce made of garlic, oregano, olive oil, lemon juice, and salt and pepper. She then made small incisions all over the meat and poured the sauce over it. Father carried the large roasting pan that held the lamb to the neighborhood bakery and paid the baker a few drachmas to cook it for us. In those days the kitchens in ordinary homes had no ovens, so cookies, bread, pastries, and roasts were taken to the neighborhood bakery to be cooked in the oven. This was very convenient for us since the lamb would be ready when we came home from church – just in time to celebrate Mother's name day.

My parents invited Olga and Andreas to celebrate with us, as well as the Armenian family who owned the fabric store. The Armenian family brought their two children, Andreana, who was ten and her brother, Chris, who was eight. Father placed a long table on the veranda where we ate our meal while overlooking the Mediterranean Sea. Andreana and I became very good friends and her brother got along well with my brothers. We were all having a wonderful time. All of a sudden we heard a noise coming from downstairs by the front gate. My parents turned around to investigate and to their surprise there stood Uncle Nicholas holding a huge basket filled with grapes in one arm and a watermelon under the other arm.

"Welcome, my brother!" said Mother, giving him a big hug. He hugged us all and whispered in my ear, "Don't say anything but I have a surprise for you children." What a wonderful surprise! We had not seen Uncle Nicholas since we moved from our village in May. We ate our dinner, washed the grapes, and sliced the watermelon Uncle Nicholas brought all the way from our village. Everyone enjoyed the wonderful dinner and fresh fruit. While the adults visited, Andreana and I played jump rope in the front yard until we became exhausted. Then I remembered that Uncle Nicholas had a surprise for us.

"Let's go and ask my uncle to show us the surprise," I said to Andreana. "Uncle Nicholas, where is our surprise? Can we see it now?"

"Close your eyes tight and I will go and bring it to you," he said. We closed our eyes and waited in anticipation. Finally, Uncle Nicholas returned and said, "Now open your eyes!" We saw a cage with three little white bunnies locked inside. He had also brought along a bundle of clover and some carrots. He told us that a mother rabbit gave birth to six little rabbits and he brought these three for my two brothers and I. We were delighted.

"This is a great gift, Uncle Nicholas, thank you, thank you!" We thanked him again with hugs and kisses on his cheek. We promised we would take good care of our bunnies.

Andreas, Olga, and the Armenian family thanked my parents for the delicious food and wonderful company and wished my mother many more years of health and happiness and said goodnight. Everyone enjoyed this day of celebration with family and new friends.

A SUMMER VISIT TO YIAYIA'S VILLAGE

My brothers and I would visit Yiayia every summer during the two weeks just before school started up again. I recall the summer of 1932. My parents put my brothers and I on a bus to travel to Yiayia's house. We felt very grown up to be traveling all alone on this journey. Yiayia was there to meet us when the bus pulled into her village of Avdou. Nothing had changed since our visit of a year before.

The narrow village streets were surfaced with cobblestones. The houses were whitewashed and most had red tile roofs but some had flat roofs made of clay and wood. The flat roofs were especially convenient in the hot summer months when people slept outdoors on the rooftop where it was cooler than inside the house. We had such fun sleeping on the roof and visiting with the neighbors who slept on the roof next door.

Yiayia was very busy that summer traveling from village to village to teach young ladies how to set their looms. Yiayia had two sisters and one of them specialized in dyeing sheep's wool and occasionally worked on special projects with Yiayia. The other sister was married and lived in her husband's village so we did not see her very often. Whenever Yiayia was away in another village, my brothers and I stayed with Polymia and Athena, our aunts.

Polymia, the oldest one, would wake us early in morning and give us bread and cheese for breakfast, then get the goat and donkey ready to go harvest the famous grapes from the valley of Avdou. In addition to dozens of varieties of grapes, Avdou was also known for its luscious melons, apples, pears, peaches, apricots, and figs. I remember one day Polymia woke us up early to start the raisin making process. As soon as we arrived at the vineyards we placed butcher paper on the ground while my aunt made a solution in which to dip the grapes. We then began picking grapes. After we collected a basketful, we dipped them into the solution and then placed them on the butcher paper to dry. We had to return to the vineyards every day to turn the grapes over and over until they became raisins.

While my brothers and I turned the grapes my aunts had to go to water the vegetable garden, which was not too far away from the vineyards. One of the ways they drew water from the well was with a device called a *shadoof.* This device has two poles in a t-shape. The horizontal pole has a bucket at one end and a counterweight at the other end. A person lowers the bucket into the well by applying their weight to the bucket side of the pole. When the bucket is filled, the person releases the pole and the counterweight raises the bucket. The pole is then swung around so that the water empties into a furrow. This method of watering, used since ancient Egyptian times, is how my aunts watered their vegetable garden. I believe this method is still in use today in some Greek villages.

I was fascinated by the *shadoof* and my aunts showed me how to let the water run from one furrow to another. When a furrow was full of water I would take a shovelful of dirt and place it to close the furrow and hold the water in. I would then open the next furrow to be watered. This process was repeated over and over again until the entire vegetable garden was watered. By the time the watering was finished I could hardly wait to go home to eat. Before watering the garden, my aunts and I had harvested some vegetables for dinner. We picked string beans, eggplant, potatoes, tomatoes, and zucchini. My Aunt Polymia used to make the best zucchini omelets I ever tasted. I was getting really hungry just thinking about it.

Aunt Polymia said it was time to leave. We followed her to a dried river that was lined on both sides with sycamore trees. We sat down on smooth stones and had a nice lunch under the shade of the sycamores. Aunt Polymia broke off several dead branches from the trees and loaded them on the donkey to use for cooking. On the way home Aunt Maria invited us to come inside her house for cold lemonade. She also invited us to stay for dinner. However, Aunt Polymia said we had to go home first to unload the wood and take a nap, as we were all very tired. She said we

would be back to have dinner later. We returned to Aunt
Maria's at eight that evening and enjoyed a delicious dinner.

After dinner we all walked to the kafenio and looked
at the bright moon over the Dict Mountains, lighting the
entire valley. George, our cousin, brought his portable
gramophone and played some popular Greek music. Before
we knew it, other young boys and girls gathered around us
and started to dance in the center of a main road that led to
another village. Of course, at night, all traffic was stopped.
We were soon ready to rest and it was past eleven when we
returned to Yiayia's. We quietly took off our shoes and
went up to the flat rooftop to sleep.

We worked hard all week long but on Sunday most
of the people in the village went to church in the morning
and to the kafenio afterwards to join their friends for
coffee and to gossip and discuss politics. After lunch most
people took afternoon naps during the midday heat. One
Sunday, my brothers and I were not tired so we decided to
play in front of Yiayia's house. We were playing jacks with
marbles and our neighbor's son, Aristadimos, joined us. He
was older than us and he was the smart aleck of the
neighborhood. On this afternoon, he sneaked up on us
with a pail of cold water and threw it at our backs,
drenching us. We chased him but he was faster than we
were and he jumped over a rock wall at the end of the
street and disappeared.

My aunts were expecting him to come over to their
house the following afternoon, so we got ready for him.
We had three pails of cold water and when he came

sneaking over to try to pull another trick on us, my aunts took hold of him and my brothers and I doused him with all three pails of water. Forty years later, my husband, children, and I would meet him in Athens. By then, that rascal was the head doctor of the pediatric department in one of the major hospitals in Athens. He invited us to his home for dinner where we met his wife, Nitsa, and his two children. We had a wonderful time reminiscing about the good old days in the little village of Avdou.

BACK HOME AGAIN

Our vacation to Yiayia's village in Avdou went by quickly. My brothers were glad to be home again. They missed Mother and Father. However, I would have liked to have stayed at Yiayia's house a bit longer, as I enjoyed being with my aunts who taught me how to do so many things. That summer, I learned how to dry grapes into raisins, how to water a huge vegetable garden, and how to dry figs on top of Yiayia's flat roof. These were all new experiences for me and I enjoyed every moment.

When we returned home to the city in the first week of September I discovered that the weather was still warm. Mother said, "Since it is so warm we should all go to the beach this Sunday to swim and to have a picnic by the sea. I will pack a basket full of sandwiches to take for lunch." My brothers and I looked forward to the swimming and picnicking with excitement.

That Sunday we arrived at the beach at about two o'clock in the afternoon. The warm sun was just right for swimming. My brothers loved the water and jumped into the sea as soon as we got there. They were both good swimmers. However, much as I loved going to the beach, I was always afraid of the water and to this day I do not know how to swim. Nonetheless, I was an expert builder of sand castles and I would compete with my brothers to see who could build the biggest castle by the sea.

When we had returned home that summer, I was surprised to discover that some changes had been made. Andreas and Olga, who lived with us, were still unable to find work, so my father hired Andreas to help with loading and unloading crates of fruits and vegetables. Also, my mother was getting very tired from her daily routine. Every morning, she would walk the long distance to our warehouse in the city and then work all day loading and unloading produce, sorting the fruits and vegetables, helping with deliveries, and working in the store. She was exhausted by the time she arrived home at night. Most of the time, she did not even have the energy to prepare dinner. Olga usually pitched in to help Mother with dinner and then she and Andreas would eat with us. Now that Andreas worked for Father, Mother could stay home with us instead.

I was delighted to have Mother stay home. We did so many things together, like cooking and shopping. When we had extra time Mother taught me how to knit and we worked on sweaters for my brothers. She was an excellent instructor but I still recall how difficult it was for me to shape a proper armhole to connect to the sleeve. I had to take it apart many times before I finally got it right.

All too soon, the fifteenth of September arrived and Mother took me to register for school. The school was approximately one mile from our house, located next to the Panagia church in the plateia. A young priest had recently installed a new bell in the bell tower of the church steeple. He liked the sound of the bell and began the custom of ringing it every hour on the hour, from dawn to dusk. Now we all had a way to tell time. The path descending to the plaza was very rocky and steep and became very slippery when it rained. For this reason, we had to go very slowly or risk breaking our necks. Many children got hurt traveling down this path and some even broke their ankles but the path never got fixed.

We met our teachers on the first day of school and they explained the rules. The school did not provide any books. These had to be purchased by parents and we were instructed to handle them with great care. My teacher introduced herself as Madam Sophia. She taught reading, writing, arithmetic, music, and handcrafts. I remember that she was very nice if you obeyed the rules but was ready to discipline with the switch she kept in her desk if you disobeyed. Another teacher, Mr. Philipos, taught us history and geography. He was also our gymnastics teacher. On Wednesdays and Fridays we walked to the *Panagia* church for religious instruction.

Andreana (the Armenian girl I met during the summer) and I became close friends. She was two years older than me and was in the fourth grade. Since my father was so busy with his new venture, he could no longer help me with my schoolwork, therefore, I asked Andreana if she could help me whenever I needed extra help with homework. She said, "Come to my house after school and I will be glad to help you."

We spent many afternoons together doing our schoolwork. She helped me whenever I got stuck. After we finished studying we would munch on feta cheese, grapes, and warm pita bread that her mother had made in a frying pan. My memories of the last days of summer and the first days of school in that year of 1932 stay with me as warm and fresh as the pita bread made by Andreana's mother.

The museum of Greek History in Iraklion.

A TRIP TO THE MUSEUM

My mother took me to school most of the time because I was afraid I would fall on the rocky path, especially if it was raining. I held my mother's hand until we got to the plaza. Once at school, if the weather were pleasant, I would play in the courtyard until the bell rang.

Once the bell rang we would assemble in a line for morning inspection before entering our classroom. Once we entered class and quieted down, the teacher greeted us and started with The Lord's Prayer. During the first section of class we had to read a story in our book. Then we had to write new words we had learned from the story over and over until we knew them by heart.

Two of my favorite subjects were history and religious education. Mr. Philipos, our history teacher, was funny and made us laugh with his jokes. He was a good instructor and by the end of the school year I remembered a lot of what he taught us. When Mr. Philip entered the classroom we all sat expectantly, our eyes trained on him, waiting to hear what he would say. Sometimes he would make witty or clever remarks that we really didn't quite understand but we thought he was funny anyway and nudged each other, giggling. One day, Mr. Philipos appeared very serious. He held up a pencil and said that it was important to know that God exists everywhere. "Even in this pencil," he said, "So if you do anything wrong you cannot hide from God. God sees you no matter where you are." One smart student raised his hand and asked, "Even if you hide under the bed?"

"Yes," the teacher answered. "Even if you hide under your bed. Consequently, if you do something wrong, you must pray and tell God you are sorry and God will forgive you."

Our next class in the day was with Mrs. Sophia, our teacher who often boasted about the city of Iraklion. "Our city has a lot to offer," she said. "One of the most important buildings in the city is the museum. So tomorrow, the entire class will take a trip to the museum. Don't forget to bring your lunch with you. If your parents wish to come, they are welcome."

I was so excited when I got home after school. I screamed to my mother as soon as I reached our front gate, "Mother, Mother! You know what? The teacher said we would all go to the museum tomorrow in Iraklion! If you like, you can come with us."

I woke the next morning jumping up and down with joy. We were going to the museum! I had no idea what the museum was all about but I was glad that I did not have to stay in class all day. It was like a holiday for me and I was delighted that my mother decided to come along. We walked the three miles to the museum, laughing and talking the entire way. Before we entered the museum our teacher said that we must all be quiet so we could listen and learn what the guide had to say. The guide met us at the door and said the first exhibit we would see was the Alexander the Great exhibit.

We walked through a corridor with both sides of the walls covered with huge pictures of famous heroes, both men and women, who fought against the Turks for Greek independence in 1821. There were also many paintings depicting famous artists and authors. One of them was El Greco (The Greek), as he was known in Spain. He was born in Crete in 1541 by the name of Domenikos Theotokopoulos. (Please don't try to pronounce the name!) Eventually he moved to Toledo, Spain and is best known for painting religious subjects.

Another famous person whose picture comes to my mind from all those years ago is Pintsentso Kornaros. He was born in Crete in 1677 and wrote the novel, *Erotokritos*, which was later made into a movie. My father loved this book and memorized entire passages. We saw portraits of many other famous Greek artists and writers that day but for some reason only these two have stayed in my mind through the years.

By the way, according to Grolier's Encyclopedia, the word *museum* comes from a Greek word meaning a grove or temple for sacred muses. The Muses were ancient Greek goddesses of art, poetry, music and science.

My mother and I enjoyed our trip to the museum. I was so happy she was able to come. We both learned so much that day and we talked about our experience for a long time afterward. I thought of my friends who still lived in the village and of all the fun we used to have together. I couldn't wait to see them again and share my experiences of life in the city and especially about my trip to the museum.

VISITING AUNT KALIOPE IN ELIA

In the fall of 1932 my mother took my brothers and I to visit her sister who lived in a small village south of Iraklion called Elia, which means olive tree in Greek. Mother had three brothers: George a policeman, Michael a stonemason, and Nicholas a farmer. She had only one sister, Kaliope. I recall riding the bus to Aunt Kaliope's village. As we rode along the bumpy roads, Mother told us the story of how Aunt Kaliope had met her husband, Alexandros. "It was a spontaneous and sincere love," said Mother.

When Aunt Kaliope was twenty-two years old she was invited to a friend's wedding in Elia. She was very beautiful. A twenty-six year old man named John saw her there for the first time and could not take his eyes off her. In fact, he wrote a song for her, which my aunt later framed and hung on her living room wall. I liked it so much that I copied it and later translated it into English as best I could. It goes like this:

Two sweet eyes drove me crazy one night
They magnetized me and took my heart away
Two kisses she gave me quickly on the lips
And from then on, I sang every night
The eyes, your own eyes
The eyes with so much sweetness
I am telling you truly
I have never found eyes
Like your sweet eyes anywhere

John was so much in love that every weekend he would travel with his friends to the village of Mohos where he would play his bouzouki and sing the song under Kaliope's window at night. They soon got married and Mother said that the wedding celebration went on for an entire week.

Finally, we reached the village of Elia and were welcomed by Aunt Kaliope along with her husband and four children who were waiting to greet us at the bus stop. The oldest daughter, Elizabeth, was a year older than me and we became lifelong friends from that day on. We corresponded for many years.

Uncle John took our suitcases and we all walked to their house that was about four blocks away. Aunt Kaliope was a good cook and prepared chicken stew with tomato sauce, rice, salad, and lots of homemade bread. Uncle John said it was the season to harvest olives. We said we would all be glad to help.

We all got up early the next morning. After breakfast,

Mother and Aunt Kaliope prepared food to take along with us for lunch while we worked in the olive orchard. Everyone had a job to do. First Uncle John stretched a burlap blanket underneath the olive tree and then he hacked the branches with a stick so that the olives would fall on the blanket. We picked up the olives that fell on the ground with our hands and dropped them into a bucket. When the bucket was full, Uncle John emptied it into sacks, which he loaded onto the donkey to be taken to the factory and crushed into olive oil. We worked hard picking up olives on our hands and knees all week long. Although we were very tired we did not mind helping Uncle John. He was full of good humor and always made us laugh with his funny stories. We finally harvested all of the olives and Uncle John delivered them to the factory.

On the last Sunday of our visit, Uncle John and Aunt Kaliope asked the priest to baptize their youngest child. Uncle John announced that the reception would be at their house and invited friends and relatives to come celebrate the occasion. We all enjoyed the party and celebrated the baptism and the good harvest as well. The next day we had to leave to return home to Iraklion.

Morning came too soon. We all had such a good time that it was very sad to say goodbye. Uncle John and Aunt Kaliope thanked us for all our help. They asked us to visit them again in summer when all the fruit would be ripe. Uncle John gave us a five-gallon container of olive oil to take home with us. He loaded the donkey with all our things and the entire family escorted us to the bus stop. We waved goodbye as the bus drove off. I noticed Mother's eyes were filled with tears and I could tell she was already missing her sister, Aunt Kaliope.

1925-14. HPAKΛEION 'Η Μητρόπολις ('Αγ. Μηνᾶς)   CANDIE La Cathédrale (St-Minas)

St. Menas Cathedral where we attended services.

A VISIT TO SAINT MENAS CATHEDRAL

On November eleventh, *Irakliotes* (people from Iraklion) celebrate the name day of Saint Menas. The largest cathedral in Iraklion is named in memory of this saint. I remember that during November of 1932 my friend Andreana's parents were talking about the festivities that were going to take place at the cathedral in Iraklion. Ekaterine, Andreana's mother, asked my parents if that we would like to accompany them to the cathedral on the day of the festival. My parents said they would be delighted to go along, as they had never seen the inside of a cathedral. For the next few days I was filled with anticipation. The day would be special because I would be with my friend, Andreana.

On the day of the festival we woke early and arrived at the cathedral at seven in the morning to make sure we had a space. Thousands of people came from all over the region to attend. The excess of people caused lines, hundreds of feet long to start forming outside the church. Each family that came to the church brought five loaves of special bread called *artoklasia*. Tables were set up in front of the church to accommodate the loaves of bread. After the Divine Liturgy the priest came out to bless the bread. He then sliced the bread and distributed it to the people.

On the way home, Andreana's father told us that the cathedral was very important to the city of Iraklion because the bishop of the church was committed to aiding people with their problems. As divorce was unthinkable, he counseled the families to preserve marriage. Also, there were no juvenile halls at that time. Instead, the Bishop provided instruction relating to youth problems. He also enforced the Ten Commandments.

In later years I witnessed bombs falling on Crete during World War Two. The cathedral survived with minimal damage. The only destruction was to the two steeples that were each adorned with glass clocks. The glass on the front of the clocks cracked from the impact but miraculously the clocks kept running.

I still remember that the overall impact of the icons in the cathedral was breathtaking. These icons have attracted visitors from all over the world. The amazing facts I learned about the cathedral that day will always be a part of me. I returned to Saint Menas Cathedral in 1971 with my family and feel blessed that I was able to share my childhood memories and the beauty of Saint Menas with them.

MY FATHER'S COAT

The first time I ever heard about communism was during the 1930s when I was about eight years old. I was older than my years, more mature than my peers and I often paid attention to the conversations of grownups. Whenever grownups gathered at the kafenio or during festivals they would express their views on politics. They talked about the difficult times. Depression had spread throughout Greece and unemployment was very high. As a result, communist ideas spread like wildfire throughout the country. Many of the poor working class people organized communist parties throughout the region of Iraklion.

Many people openly expressed their communist ideology as being good for the working class because everything would be divided equally. The communist ideas spread from town to town, from village to village. However, the Greek people were ninety-eight percent Orthodox Christian and our religious leaders opposed communism because they thought that it would destroy Christianity.

The harsh winter of 1933 is permanently frozen in
my mind. It was a frigid January with temperatures in the
thirties and winds so strong that fifty-foot waves rolled in
from the sea and completely covered the harbor. It was so
cold that my teeth chattered when I would walk to school.
During that same January, the Communist party started a
revolt. Thousands of working class people who had no
hope of improving their living conditions began rioting in
several places within the city. Fighting took place from
behind walls, trees, and buildings. Intermittent street
fighting was going on in different parts of the city.
Gunshots could be heard throughout the town. Some
people were killed as they walked down the street. The
government sent soldiers to stop the fighting but it
continued for weeks. My father was drafted to help fight
the communist party in Greece. This was the second time
he served in the Hellenic Army. Just ten years earlier he was
a prisoner of war during the Turkish conflict with Greece
in 1923.

While the rioting continued, nearly all of the
commercial buildings closed. The bakery did not bake
bread and the grocery store closed. We had no food in the
house except for flour. Mother made pita bread every day,
which we dipped in a dish of vinegar mixed with olive oil.
This was our diet for many weeks. As a result, we became
constipated and Mother had to give us castor oil. How my
brothers and I hated that taste, but we had no choice but to
swallow it.

The fighting continued. The communists killed the

guards and took over City Hall. It seemed like war was breaking out all over the city. After a month, the fighting finally came to an end. However, many people were killed on both sides and many others were wounded. The frigid weather persisted even after the fighting ended.

When my father was finally released from the military, he came home wearing a military coat. He said to my mother, "Business is not doing so well and I have no money to buy a coat to keep myself warm, so I think I'll keep this one. The army will never miss it."

A few days later, there were rumors that the army police were searching the homes of men who did not return their military uniforms. Father decided to keep the coat anyway. He put it in a burlap sack, tied it with a wire, secured it with a hook, and then hung it inside the chimney while a fire was slowly burning.

A few mornings later, I looked out the window and saw the military police marching down the street toward our house. I quickly climbed the stairs two at a time, ran into my mother's room, and pulled a blanket from her bed. I wrapped myself up in the blanket and hid under the bed, shaking with fright. My heart beat so fast that I thought it would jump right out of my chest. I began to pray, repeating The Lord's Prayer over and over, trying to calm myself. I could hear the police searching downstairs. I was praying hard to God, "Please don't let them find the coat and put my father in jail."

Then I heard them tromping up the steps, coming closer. I prayed harder. They pushed the door open and began searching the room, pulling drawers open, looking in closets, and lifting mattresses from the beds and looking under them. They lifted my mother's mattress and found me under the bed. My face was covered with the blanket. They pulled it back and asked what I was doing under the bed. Thinking quickly, I said the first thing that came to my mind. "I'm hiding from my brothers," I replied. I guess they believed me. They left the room laughing and muttering about children and their games.

As soon as they left, my mother came looking for me. I came out of my hiding place still shaking with fright. I collapsed into my mother's arms sobbing, "What happened to Father? Are the police going to take him away?" She held me and tried to calm me, saying not to worry, everything would be fine. Father was safe.

Days went by and I forgot all about the coat. One afternoon, when I came home from school, I saw Mother with the coat spread over her lap, cutting the brass buttons off. She cut the belt off the back of the coat. The following day she dyed the coat black and kept it inside the house to until it dried. Then Mother took the coat from the hanger and sewed plain black buttons on it. Father wore that coat for the remainder of the winter and no one noticed the change. I still remember sitting in school and thinking that one day I would come home and find out that the military police had taken my father away. I will never forget that January of 1933, the cold and fear never left me.

UNCLE GEORGE TAKES A CHANCE

In September of 1933, my father received a letter from my Uncle George asking him to bring our family to help harvest grapes. During this time, my father's business was hit hard by the depression. Since business was so slow, he asked my mother if she would like to go help with the harvest. Uncle George would have reliable help and Mother could earn some money to pay the bills. My mother was delighted to go, as she had not seen her brother in a long time. Mother packed her clothes and our entire family was soon on the bus heading toward Uncle George's vineyard.

Uncle George first planted the vines early in the spring of 1928. I recall the story told to me by my father of how Uncle George acquired the land for his vineyard:

"In a broad valley south of Iraklion there is a village called Harakas. One day, Uncle George was reading his newspaper and saw an ad under a government listing that stated that there were ten acres of wasteland for sale in the village of Harakas. Any citizen over the age of twenty-one could apply for possession of this land. It said to write to the Agriculture Department for more information. Since George had six children he thought that acquiring this land would be a good investment for the future. He came to our house and asked me to go with him to inspect this property. When we returned, I told Mother that the land was full of sagebrush and thorn bushes. I did not think it would be worth the time or hard labor involved to prepare the land for use. George thought and thought about whether or not to buy this property. He made a decision and came to tell me. 'I will never have another opportunity like this one,' he said. 'I will go tomorrow to the Agriculture Department and get more information.'

He spoke with the agriculture officials and immediately filed to acquire the property. The government official told him that if he paid one dollar an acre, he could have the property immediately. He gladly paid the ten drachmas and got a paper with a description of the property and a receipt showing that he paid for the land in full."

My uncle George was almost six feet tall and very muscular. His oldest son, Michael, was sixteen and as tall as his father. They looked alike and had light brown hair and greenish eyes. People said that they were a handsome pair. My uncle dreamed that by acquiring this land he could teach his son to become a good wine maker. He planned to clear the ten acres and plant a vineyard.

In the spring of 1928, Uncle George took his family to Harakas where he built a temporary shelter to live in while clearing the property. The family began clearing the property with picks and shovels. It took all summer to clear the land. Father said we had been there helping Uncle George, but I was too young to remember the event. Uncle George ploughed the ground using oxen and planted his vines.

Now, five and a half years later, the vines were heavy with grapes and ready for harvest. I was so happy that my brothers and I did not have school during these first two weeks of September, so that we were able to travel to meet our cousins for the very first time. Because we were lacked money and transportation we did not get to see our relatives very often. This was a significant trip for us. We arrived in the afternoon and Uncle George met us at the bus stop. He hugged my mother. He said, "I am sure glad to see you all. The children did not come with me. They are busy preparing the gear we need for tomorrow. We will see them soon."

When we reached the house, our relatives surrounded us and gave us hugs. Aunt Maria, Uncle George' wife, said, "Sit down. I have made fresh lemonade for you and dinner will be ready in an hour." While waiting for dinner, we stepped outside and admired the vines, heavy with grapes. We sampled a few of the luscious grapes and Uncle George told us to pick some Muscat grapes to have after dinner. "While you do that," he said, "I'll go cut some melons that I grew behind my shelter. You'll like them, too. They are very sweet."

Aunt Maria set a long table with plates for all. In the middle was a big kettle filled with lamb stew, a bowl of salad, olives and bread. We sat around the table eating and talking. Finally, Uncle George said, "We better go to bed early, as we all have a lot of work to do tomorrow."

The next morning we all got up early, had some bread and cheese for breakfast, and went straight to work. We all helped cut the grapes and load the baskets. My father and Uncle George loaded the baskets into a horse-drawn wagon and took the grapes into town to be processed. Grape juice was put into barrels and took six months to become wine. When it was ready, Uncle George bottled it and glued on a label. It was called, *George and Son Michael*. In the first year they sold the wine locally. As the years went by, his wines grew in popularity. People liked his wines because of his commitment to organic grape growing and natural wine making, which resulted in distinctive wines that tasted fresh and fruity. His specialty was a wine similar to merlot that went well with spicy sausages, meat loaves, stews, and casseroles. Most of his wines were sold to tourists who came from all over the world.

Uncle George continued making wine for many years, hoping to pass the business down to his son, Michael. Michael, however, had other dreams and married a nice young lady from the nearby village of Pyros when he was twenty-five years old. Ten years later he applied for a government job and became a federal agent in Athens.

STRUGGLING TO SURVIVE

The 1930s were hard for my family. Father's fruit and vegetable business came to a standstill. Olga and Andreas, the couple who lived and worked with us, moved to Salonika after hearing from a friend that Andreas could find a job doing construction work there.

When Father's business first began to fail he started having dark moods. He stayed out late at night and often did not come home until after midnight. He did not have a strong sense of purpose about life and his outlook was one of hopelessness. During this financial crisis, it was very difficult to find work. Father no longer took responsibility for himself or for his family. He was only interested in traveling from place to place and in playing cards with his friends. We struggled to stay alive. Occasionally, if one of Father's odd jobs came through or if he won some money gambling (which was rare) then we would have food to eat for a few weeks. However, the food would soon be gone and we would be hungry once again. As time passed and we continued in our hunger, Father promised that *one of these days* he would hit a jackpot and we would all be rich.

However, that type of wishful thinking never became a reality.

I remember one night when Father *did* come home with his pockets full of money. He emptied the money onto the kitchen table and asked my brothers and I to help him sort out the change. We eagerly gathered around the table and sorted all the coins into various piles according to the denomination. In the morning, Father planned to take all the coins to the bank in order to exchange them for bills. My mother went with him in order to convince him to give her some money for groceries. He gave her enough money to last us a month. That was the first time my brothers and I saw that much money. We were overwhelmed and thought that we had suddenly become rich, just as father had promised.

The days flew by. We hadn't seen Father for weeks. Mother began to worry and became depressed. She went to the city to look for him. She inquired at the kafenio, asking if anyone had seen him. One of the owners said he had seen him the night before, playing cards across the street. Mother returned home to fix dinner for us. After dinner she said, "I am going to look for your father at the kafenio. Do not worry. Go to bed when you finish your schoolwork. I will be back as soon as I find your father." I was eight years old at the time and I was very worried about my mother. She cried every night after we went to bed. She looked years older than her age.

Mother finally returned around midnight and had Father with her. I had been unable to fall asleep and was still awake when they came home. I heard them arguing about how much money he had lost playing cards. Mother was very angry at the way he behaved and was upset because he did not worry about his children and their future. I heard her say that we were better off when we lived in the village, where we always had food on the table.

A few days after that night, Father came home late one evening and said, "Get ready to move. We have to leave. We can no longer live in this house." We were scared and did not understand what happened or why we had to leave our house. Mother started to cry and asked Father why we had to move. He said that he borrowed money to bet on a jackpot but lost the bet. The man who loaned him the money offered to buy our house for whatever equity was left. Mother was devastated. She could not believe what she was hearing. She almost fainted. I remember bracing her so that she would not fall on the cement floor and hurt herself. We were all sad and crying. My brothers and I hugged each other.

Father hired a pickup truck and brought over a couple of friends to load the bedroom furniture. "Don't cry," he said, "I have enough money and bought us a pre-fab building and erected it on government land in the outskirts of the city. That's where we are going to tonight."

We left the city and came to a two-mile stretch of land set against a Venetian fortress wall that had been built in medieval times. Rows of neglected looking, flat-roofed, plywood buildings covered with stucco appeared before us. Most of the people who lived on this two-mile long piece of land were either disabled veterans or widows from World War One. Many of them had been there for years.

By the time we reached our building it was almost midnight and we were physically and emotionally exhausted. Father and his friends unloaded our mattresses and set them atop cardboard boxes on the dirty floor. We fell onto them fully clothed. We were too shocked to sleep. There was a knock on the door and a policeman entered. "Do you have a permit to erect this building on this property?" he asked my father.

Father answered that he did not have a permit. He thought there was a law exempting families with children who had nowhere else to go. The policeman stated that that particular exemption expired two years earlier. The policeman looked down at my brothers and I with compassion in his heart. We were huddled together, frightened and crying. He said, "I feel very sorry for your children. Tomorrow, I will appeal to the city mayor on your behalf and perhaps I can get a permit for you."

My father thanked him and told him how much he appreciated his help. "I hope you can get a permit for me," he said, "I have no other place to take my children." My father had no work and no money to rent a house for his family. He felt very bad about losing our house through his gambling.

My mother became very depressed about losing the house. The property in Mohos had been part of the inheritance my mother received from her parents, who worked all their lives to provide for their descendants. I remind myself that life is like climbing a mountain. You painstakingly ascend to the top but you must still be careful to not go too fast when you ascend, or you may fall and harm yourself. I wish some things in my life's story had worked out differently, but we cannot change the past and most of the time we cannot control the future. Nevertheless, this is the experience of my life and I am trying to express it as best as I can.

The next day the policeman returned to our house. He told my father that he presented our family's situation to the mayor. Since the mayor had known the policeman for a very long time, he had confidence in his judgment and knew that he always spoke the truth. The mayor agreed to issue a permit allowing our family to stay on the government property. The policeman promised, "It will be a week or so before the permit is ready. Do not worry. I will bring it to you in person." My parents thanked him with tears streaming down their cheeks. They gave the policeman big hugs and said, "God bless you. We will never forget you for as long as we live." The policeman said his name was Haralambos Thaskalakis. We eagerly awaited his return.

Meanwhile, we had time to survey the area where we now lived. Across the street was a machine shop that made noise from morning until late at night. Down the street was a leather tannery and three blocks down and across the street was an avenue lined with raisin factories. On the other side of the fortress wall there was a military base where cadets trained in an area as large as a football stadium.

Since there was so much activity all around us my father decided to open a coffee shop. He divided our building into two areas. One half was our living quarters and contained two bedrooms while the other half became the coffee shop. Father built a large storefront window. He built a twenty-four by twenty-four foot frame that he then covered with bamboo to shade the area. He painted the building white and made a sign that said *Manoli's Café* and nailed it up in front of the coffee shop.

Across one wall of the coffee shop's interior he built a long counter with cabinets to hold cups, glasses, and other supplies. He then went to a second-hand store and bought four round metal tables and sixteen chairs. He placed these around the shaded patio so that patrons could sit in the shade during the hot summer months and enjoy a nice cup of coffee. My father taught me how to make the coffee and wrote the instructions on a piece of paper that he pinned to the cupboard so I could read the formula.

Because the counter was too high for me, Father built a stool I could stand on to prepare the coffee on the burner. When Mother saw how nice everything looked she wanted to add some special touches. She planted honeysuckle on each column of the patio to create a trellis. My father decided to have a grand opening party. He invited some of the business people and Haralambos, the Policeman, as well as my friend, Andreana, and her family. Mother made *souvlakia, spanakopita*, and *tiropita* for the occasion. Father wanted the celebration to be joyful for everyone, especially his family, because he felt so bad about losing our house and not being a stable provider.

It wasn't until much later in life that I began to understand why my father was so unstable in his life. Fighting in two wars, being taken as a prisoner of war in the 1920s, and then battling the communists in the 1930s took a toll on both his spirit and his ability to provide. I often think about the hardships my parents endured as I sip a cup of coffee prepared in the same way my father taught me so many years ago.

Haralambos remained a life-long family friend and even baptized my little sister. Years later, my family and I visited Haralambos and his family in Crete. After he retired from the police department he became a baker. My husband Floyd helped him deliver his bread during our vacation to Crete.

OUR COFFEE SHOP

It was early in June of 1934 when my father opened his coffee shop. In early spring anemones of various colors grew on top of the fortress wall and rows of red, white, and pink oleander grew along the sides of the wall along with wild roses, which filled the air with fragrance. My brothers and I picked the flowers and brought them to my mother. She put them in small vases and placed them on the tables underneath the shade of the kafenio patio.

The first customer arrived around noon. It was Mr. Constantine from the machine shop. Father said that Mr. Constantine did the best wrought iron work. As word of his fine workmanship got around, he received orders from other towns with his fame traveling as far as the island of Santorini. He had blue eyes and light colored hair. His hands were always greasy and his clothing was very black. I think he would have been a good-looking man if he had cleaned up. He was very polite and always gave me a tip when I served him coffee. Today, he asked my father for the lunch specials. Father said, "I just started to barbecue some pork chops. How does that sound to you?"

"My partner will be joining me, so make that two orders with french fries, salads, and wine," Mr. Constantine replied.

The aroma of pork chops permeated the air all the way across the street. By the time they were just about finished cooking, all the tables were filled of customers. Our whole family loved our coffee shop. We were well organized and all worked well together. My brother, Antonti, served the water. My job was to make the coffee. Mother continuously cooked french fries and made salads while Father barbecued the chops. Father changed the menu every day. When fresh fish was available he cooked it over the barbecue grill.

The soldiers from the army base often came in the evenings. They would sit under the patio, sipping ouzo and enjoying the feta cheese, sliced tomatoes, cucumbers, and *kalamata* olives that my mother served them. My father knew how to entertain people. His jokes and funny stories always made everyone laugh. Sometimes he would recite from *Erotokritos* to change the mood of the people. But the main highlight of the evening was always the performance of my younger brother Eleftherios. He loved to dance and loved the public attention. My father played a flute made of bamboo while my brother danced the Cretan dance, *pentozaly*. He would finish with a spirited *opa!* as he lifted his knees high in an impromptu flourish. After he finished dancing the customers would clap and give him a small tip. When the next night arrived my brother would dance all over again.

One evening, Father surprised us with an old phonograph. It was the first time I had ever seen anything like this. It had a horn that looked like a morning glory flower. Father said that it played music. I was amazed that a morning glory could play music. Father smiled and said, "Wait, you will see." He put a round disc in it and turned the handle to make it play. I could not believe my ears. It was magic to me. Whenever Father was busy at the barbecue he would place a record in the phonograph and my brother would dance the *pentozaly* to the music.

At about three in the afternoon the people who worked in the offices across the street would order Greek coffee. My father made the coffee and I delivered the first order. By the time I returned the next order was ready to go. I carried coffee and water to our customers in a tri-pot tray. My father told me to be careful not to spill the coffee as I walked across the street. "You may get a good tip if everything looks good," he would say. Most of the time I delivered the coffee without spilling any of it.

One of our steady customers, Mr. Xenofon, always dressed in a white shirt and dark trousers. He was always good to me and tipped me every time I delivered his coffee. I also delivered coffee to the ladies who worked in the raisin factories. The inside of the factory was bright and had a lot of windows. There were tables lines side by side in a row about one hundred feet long with benches on either side where the ladies sat. A conveyor belt sorted the raisins from the stems and then poured them into wooden boxes.

The ladies emptied the boxes onto the long tables and sorted out the bad raisins from the good. The raisins were cleaned and packed for markets abroad. They were shipped to Europe and even America.

Things were going well at the coffee shop. My family did not make a lot of money but we had food to eat whenever we were hungry. I enjoyed working in the kafenio. Eventually I learned how to make Greek coffee without reading the directions. What I learned at the kafenio at a young age was useful to me many years later in another country when I was chairman for the kafenio at the Saint Nicholas Greek Food Festival in California. My customers said that I made the best coffee and I could feel my father smiling down at me. Some of the customers finished their coffee and asked me if I could read their fortune from the cup. I always wished that I had this talent and thought of making up some funny stories, but that would not be truthful. Anyway, I do not believe in fortune telling but I will tell you a true story that made me wonder about it.

When my family and I were in Athens in 1971, my husband and I, along with our daughter Marie and son David, visited my cousin, Michael, the one who became a federal investigator. At that time, Michael had three children who were close in age to our children. They all got along very well and had a lot of fun playing puppet shows together. We stayed with them for several days and enjoyed talking about the olden days when my uncle made wine in the village. While we were visiting cousin Michael, we met his mother-in-law, a widow from the town of Smyrna. She was a refugee from the Greek-Turkish conflict that occurred in the 1920s. Her husband was killed in that war.

One afternoon, we enjoyed some delicious *koulourakia* and coffee that she prepared for us. When I finished my coffee, she asked if I would like to have her read my cup. She knew how to read a cup. In fact, people came from all over and paid her to read their cups. Mainly out of curiosity, I told her I would like that. I turned my cup upside down on the saucer and waited for the dregs to drain. A few minutes later, she lifted my cup and began to study it.

She said, "When you return to America you will have a court trial. A man embezzled a lot of money from you. He will lose the case and you will recover most of your money." I could not believe what she was saying. My husband and I were both amazed at what we heard. How could she know what was going on in our lives so far away in America? I had never written to any of my relatives about this case, nor had we discussed it with anyone. What she said puzzles me to this day. However, everything she told us came true. We went through an agonizing period but we did recover most of our money. It taught us a lesson not to trust anyone but that's another story. Let's go back to the kafenio.

That summer of 1934, my aunts, Polymia and Athena, came to Iraklion. They rented a room near us and found work in the raisin factory. They worked every day except Sunday. They worked hard all summer and made very good wages. When fall came and it was time to go back to the village, they both went shopping and bought yards and yards of white cotton material to make bed sheets and pillowcases for their dowry. We usually spent Sunday afternoons together.

I remember one Sunday evening when my Yiayia offered to fix dinner. She mixed a sauce and marinated steak in it. It was a very large steak, big enough for all of us. She placed it in a dish and left it on the counter to soak in the delicious seasonings while she went outside to light a fire in the barbecue. I was just coming in through the door to help Yiayia when I saw my brother's cat pulling the chunk of meat onto the dirty floor. I pounced on him in a fit of rage but it was too late. My Yiayia was upset because that devil of a cat was going to make the whole family go hungry. All Yiayia wanted was to catch the thief, tie a stone around his neck, and fling him into the sea. My father became so angry that on the following day he took the cat, put him in a sack, and told my brothers, "Take him to the sea and shove him into the water."

But guess what? The next day the cat was back in our coffee shop. Three times my brothers took the cat to the sea and the cat always came back. I really think that they did not want to drown the cat.

One day my father went to the village to buy fresh produce for the kafenio, so he took the cat with him and left it in the village. When he returned he brought us a new pet: a young pig. He said, "We have lots of scraps left over from salads and potato peelings to fatten up this pig to have him for Christmas dinner." My brothers were really happy to have a new pet. Our pig became so friendly and we eventually built a corral to keep him from wandering around.

AFTERNOON AT THE SEA

On one warm summer afternoon my parents allowed Yiayia and Athena to take my brothers and I to the sea. Our pig had become so friendly that he followed us all the way to the sea. We walked on a paved road for two miles with the smell of saltwater becoming more pervasive as we came closer to the sea. Eventually, we came to a cliff above the sea where we would find a sandy path that descended to the sandbar.

Yiayia, did not know how to swim but she enjoyed wading in the water. She always wore black from head to toe, as she was a widow. When she went to the ocean with us she would leave her stockings behind and wear wooden sandals to the beach. When she arrived she would then be able to gather her ankle length skirt, draw it to one side, and tuck it into the waist. The rest of us would wear our undergarments. The sea was like glass here and there was no waves. The water was so shallow that you could walk out into the ocean two hundred feet and it would only be up to your waist.

None of us knew how to swim, except for our pet pig. He knew how to swim better than any of us. We would laugh at the site of him running on the seashore oinking. My brothers and I had fun jumping in the water and splashing each other. Once in a while we would get a taste of the salt water in our mouths. The sea was so refreshing; it somehow washed away our thoughts of work and worry and allowed our childish hearts to be carefree in the summer sun. After a few hours we needed to return to help our parents for the dinner hour back at the kafenio. As soon as we started to leave, our pet pig, which we came to love, followed after us oinking as if to say, "Hey, wait for me!"

When we arrived at the coffee shop, we found that some of the soldiers from the military base had come for dinner. Father had been expecting us and had offered them a cold drink of *Gazoza* (a drink that tastes like 7-Up), hoping to stall them until we got there to help with dinner. Father said to us, "Hurry, these men are hungry for dinner and mother and I need your help!" We quickly went inside to change and come to the rescue. Yiayia jumped in immediately, as she already had her clothes on. She quickly brought them some ouzo and cucumbers to get by on and then went to help my mother.

The soldiers were always nice to us. Some of them had become regular customers and knew us by name, "Yiassou Aristea, yiassou Michael, yiassou Eleftherios". Yiayia tended to keep Athena inside and occupied cooking, as she did not want her to get too close to any of the soldiers. Sometimes, for a treat, the soldiers would bring us some rose flavored Greek Loukoumi with almonds or walnuts inside. We all enjoyed that. My mother prepared some shish kabob and vegetarian stew. After being at the ocean our appetites were the size of Poseidon and the smell of the shish kabob grilling on the barbeque floated in the air, tantalizing our noses, tongues, and stomachs. Father and Mother were happy to have their kafenio filled with customers.

Finally, Mother and Yiayia heaped the table with shish kabobs, mixed vegetable casserole, homemade bread, a village salad, and feta cheese. My parents let us sit at another table close by so that we could also enjoy the freshly cooked dinner. My father would sometimes sit down with the soldiers who welcomed his presence, saying "Come, Kyrios Manolis, tell us one of your stories." They were interested to hear my father tell them stories about the Turkish War in 1922.

Yiayia told the soldiers her story about how her husband had been in America before the World War One and how he returned in the late 1920s and died of tuberculosis. Yiayia remained a widow. In those days, we believed that marriage was for life. Women married their men for life, whether the man lived or died. It was uncommon for any widow to remarry.

After dinner, Father turned on the morning glory phonograph and my brother, Eleftherios, danced the Cretan Pentozaly. When he was finished, everyone clapped and the soldiers gave him a small tip. Occasionally they gave me a tip as well, just enough to enjoy buying a little candy at the *periptero* (kiosk).

A few of the soldiers who played instruments would bring them on occasion and play for us. Our neighbors down the street, Aleko and Anna, would hear the bouzouki and come to join us. They were sister and brother and close in age to my brothers and I. Their mother, Toula, was a nurse who worked in an orphanage on the outskirts of Iraklion. Their grandmother lived with them. Both mother and grandmother were widows. I don't recall what happened to their husbands. We became good friends with Aleko and Anna and we walked to school together. We remained friends for many years, even writing after I came to America.

We all enjoyed that summer evening and the soldiers thanked us for the delicious food and entertainment. We said "It was our pleasure and goodnight until next time." We then helped to clear the tables to be ready for tomorrow's customers.

Once in a blue moon, when the coffee shop was closed on Sunday, my parents would take us to the plaza in town where there was a beautiful water fountain, called *The Lion's Fountain,* which still flows today. It was erected some time during the Venetian occupation of Crete from 1204 to 1669 CE. We would go to a restaurant there where my father knew the owner to have dessert for a special treat. My favorite was *galaktoboureko,* filo dough filled with custard and baked in the oven with a lemon syrup drizzled on top.

THREE WISEMEN

The fall of 1935 came quickly. My brothers and I attended Holy Trinity School. Aleko and his sister Anna also attended Holy Trinity and we walked to school together every day. A program from the Red Cross provided lunch for underprivileged children, so we had lunch at school every day. I was glad we ate there because my mother did not feel well sometimes. I knew something was wrong with my mother when I heard her tell Athena she was pregnant.

In November we began the forty-day fast prior to Christmas. My mother was sick and unable to cook. As a result, the kafenio was not doing very well and the family was suffering financially. The factory closed for the winter and Yiayia and Athena had gone back to the village, so mother did not have much help.

One weekend, Andreana's mother, Ekaterina came to visit my mother. She noticed that my mother was depressed and wanted to lift her spirits by inviting her over for a visit. When my mother went to visit Ekaterina, she had a great idea to dress her son, Christ, and my two brothers the

Three Wise Men to go caroling the week before Christmas.

My mother, my brothers, and I went to Ekaterina's house the following weekend to work on the project. Ekaterina supplied us with some bright fabric remnants from the fabric store they owned. We worked together for three weekends. We enjoyed making the costumes and each other's company. When we finished, the boys tried on their costumes. They fit perfectly and the gold, blue, and maroon colors complimented each other stunningly. The boys were delighted and so were we. The boys were ready to go caroling when it was time.

Christmas was approaching and the days became colder. It rained almost every day. During the forty days before Christmas there is a church service every evening. The church bells rang, calling us to attend the vespers service, reminding us that Christmas would be here soon.

My Aunt Kaliope was a very devout churchgoer. If she could, she would be in church every evening. However, she had to work occasionally at the nursing home at night to help feed older people who could not feed themselves.

One Saturday evening when Theia Kaliope was not working and I was very bored staying at home, she asked me, "Aristea, would you like to go to church with me?" I was anxious to get out and have a change of atmosphere so I said I would go. The church was near her house so we did not have very far to walk. As soon as we entered the church, even though I was a young child, I felt within me a deep reverence for God. I was at home in the church, feeling that the Holy Spirit was upon me and that the presence of Christ, Panagia and the saints was near. The smell of the beeswax candles and incense burning struck me and reminded me of the holy presence of God. I could not articulate my vivid church experience then, as I do now. It was rich.

After the services, Aunt Kaliope invited me to have some lentil soup, bread, and olives at her home. She was an excellent cook. After dinner she offered me some hot tea. Feeling the warmth of her love and hospitality, I returned home with a renewed spirit.

A week before Christmas, it was time for the boys to go caroling. It was a tradition for the children to carry a basket of cookies from house to house while singing Christmas carols. While the boys were caroling, we decorated our Christmas tree with homemade decorations. There were not many pine trees so we could not cut down an entire tree. Instead, we cut a large branch from a pine tree and made that our Christmas tree. I remember it was entertaining. I helped Andreana by making angels from white organdy material and necklaces from acorn nuts. We made chains from colored paper and icicles from cigarette packages and candy wrappers. When we finished decorating our pine branch, it was beautiful. Our neighbors were so surprised to see the boys dressed as the Three Kings and the boys were so delighted by the generosity of the people. They came home to show us their baskets filled with nuts, raisins, cookies, and candy.

Athena came from the village a few days before Christmas to celebrate the holidays with the family.

Christmas is a day of worship, radiant with joy and the wonder of the birth of Jesus. On Christmas Eve, we went to church with Efthihia's family. After the service, Ekaterina invited us to her house for *avgolemo* (traditional chicken-lemon soup). She surprised us with delicious *galaktoboureko* dessert that her husband had purchased at the pastry shop. We ate it with great delight and thanked him for the special treat. We sang carols and had a wonderful evening.

SCHOOL PROJECT

After the Christmas holiday school began again. I enjoyed going to school with my brothers Michael and Eleftherios. Out friends, Aleko and Anna walked to school with us. No matter where we went, we walked. There weren't school buses in those days. As I recall there weren't any city buses either. The only bus available was from the city to various villages.

My brothers and our friends loved to walk to school. On the way to school they would find a lot of ways to amuse themselves. If there were any stray dogs on the way, they would urge them to follow us all the way to school. There were many stray dogs on the streets, as many of the owners didn't keep them in their yards. Many of the yards were open.

School was very important to me and I tried to study hard to maintain good grades. Our main subjects were reading, writing, arithmetic, geography, and history. We also had music and religious studies twice a week.

When the weather permitted we had gymnastics as well

as lessons in handcrafts and embroidery. During recess we
played jacks with pebbles we gathered at the seashore,
hopscotch, tag, and double jump rope. We also created
games ourselves, such as checkers made by drawing squares
on cardboard. We also played marbles, hide-the-button,
and catch-the-wolf. I became so good at playing checkers
that I would beat every student that played with me. The
worst thing was when they didn't want to play with me
anymore. So I devised a strategy to let them win the first
game.

I remember that in the winter of 1936 our teacher
assigned us a sailboat project. The boys were to make the
frame and the girls made the sails. We calculated the
needed length and width and drew a blueprint on paper.
The boys went around the neighborhood to ask people for
scraps of wood. Mr. Niko, who lived next door to our
home, was a carpenter. We asked him if he would help us
saw the boards to size. He said that he was glad to help us
with the project.

One afternoon, Mr. Niko came to the school and
sawed the boards as the girls worked on designing the sails.
We cut out the material according to the design on the
paper. However, we discovered that the sailcloth was heavy
and too difficult to sew by hand. So we decided to take it to
a tailor's shop instead. When we told the owner that it was
for a school project he was glad to sew the sails for us. He
said, "Leave the material with me and come back in a
couple of days and I will have it ready for you."

Everything was coming along wonderfully and our

teacher was pleased with the results. The boys, with the help of Mr. Niko, nailed the boards onto the posts. When the framework was finished we filled the joints with tar to seal the cracks so that water couldn't get in. When we had finished the framework and sealed the joints, we took our time varnishing the outside of the sailboat. We applied several coats of varnish. After each application we had to let it dry for a couple of days before we applied the next one. The class worked almost all winter on the project.

I was so disappointed because I could not help much with the project. I had to help my mother with house chores, as she was pregnant and she was not feeling well most of the time. However, I helped as much as I could and I was very proud to be a part of the assignment.

When the boat was ready, Mr. Niko installed the sails. He also made two oars for the boat to steer it to shore in case the wind didn't cooperate. We were excited and eager to see the finished product. Finally, the boat was ready to be put into the water. What an exciting moment this was, we could hardly wait to try the boat out. Mr. Niko came with an open wagon pulled by a horse. He loaded the sailboat into the wagon and drove it to the sea, while the whole class walked behind.

It was a beautiful warm day close to the end of April. The sky was crystal clear and various colors of daisies were in bloom among the rocks. We walked to the sea and Mr. Niko placed the sailboat in the water. Then he got in the boat and navigated it around for a few miles. Everything was working magnificently he told us. The boat was big enough for two people so he took us one at a time for a ride. He let us steer it with oars because there was not enough wind to move the boat.

It was marvelous to see our sailboat floating on the water like a white swan. We spent the whole day by the sea admiring our boat and enjoying the rides. What an unforgettable day that was! We felt proud of ourselves and were amazed at our accomplishment. At the end of the school year there was a handcraft exhibit for all the schools in the city. Our teacher advised us to enter our boat in the exhibit. We displayed it on a table and wrote on a piece of paper, *Holy Trinity School Project of the Fourth Grade.* We were very surprised when the judges gave us an award for first prize. That memorable event stayed with me for many years as my classmates and I bragged about our sailboat.

MY SISTER'S BAPTISM

School was over and summer break began. My father put us to work at the kafenio with my brothers cleaning tables and serving the customers water while I was busy making the coffee. One evening some of the soldiers came for dinner and I remember overhearing my father speaking with them and asking, "So do you think that there will be another war?"

"We are not sure but we have to be prepared."

We had our own battles to fight so I did not pay much attention. My mother gave birth to a baby girl, Georgia, in May, so she was unable to help at the kafenio. Father sent a letter to Athena and Yiayia asking them if they would come help Mother with the baby before the raisin factory opened for the summer. They came the following week.

It was eleven in the morning when they arrived at the bus stop and they were tired from the trip. Athena said, "We have to go see if the rental room is ready and rest for a while." So father helped them with their luggage as they walked the few blocks to the boardinghouse.

Yiayia finally came to help my mother with the baby in the earlier part of the afternoon. The baby was very fussy during the night and Mother couldn't get much sleep. Around five, father started barbequing pork chops for dinner while Yiayia cooked french fries and made a huge salad. Athena arrived around next. She was dressed in a light blue dress and looked incredibly beautiful with her huge dark eyes and wavy chestnut hair. Yiayia called us for dinner and we all enjoyed the pork chops and the french fries. After dinner Yiayia made coffee while Athena served *bougatsa* she had made early that afternoon. Everyone praised her for the delicious dessert.

The baby woke up and my brother, Michael, brought her in to show his baby sister to everyone. Her cheeks were pink like roses and he gave her to Aunt Athena, who exclaimed, "She is so cute, Maria, she looks like you!"

My brothers and I were so happy to have a little sister. We took turns taking care of her – rocking her to sleep, changing her diapers, and giving her baths. Mother was tired most of the time and the baby kept waking her up at night, so we told her, "Mother, we will take care of her if she wakes up at night." My mother seemed to be having a difficult time regaining her strength. "Thank you children," my mother replied, "That would be a tremendous help to me."

It was June when our friend, Mr. Haralambos, came to visit our family. He was the policeman who helped my father obtain a building permit for the kafenio. He congratulated my parents on Georgia and asked if he could be the godfather when she was baptized. His offer was gladly accepted and they set the date of the baptism for August twenty-fifth, provided that the priest was available on that day.

The next day, Father went to the church and made the arrangements. When August twenty-fifth came, Yiayia and Athena offered to prepare the food for the guests – some thirty people. They came over to the kafenio and made tiropites, pastitsio, meatballs, stuffed grape leaves, and horiatiki salad. For dessert they made baklava. We helped father arrange the tables and chairs on the patio and everything was ready before we went to the church.

The church ceremony was magnificent. When we returned to the kafenio, Yiayia served the food while father filled the glasses with wine. He raised his glass to good health and happiness to all and he made a special toast to Mr. Haralambos for being the godfather. He also expressed his thanks and gratitude to Yiayia and Athena for the tasty and delicious meal. Father said to his sister, "When you get married you will satisfy your husband well with your excellent cooking and delicious meals."

LOSING MY MOTHER

After my mother gave birth to my sister, Georgia, it was obvious that she was not well. She slowly fell into a depression. She got worse every day. She became more irritable and it became difficult to reason with her. Most of the time, she was confused, depressed, and disorganized. It became impossible for my father to continue to operate the kafenio because of her unpredictable behavior. He had to close the shop.

She began to run through the streets at night. Sometimes she would go across the street to the machine shop and beat the huge metal tanks with stones. She made so much noise that she would wake up the entire neighborhood. She slept on the Venetian stonewall behind the kafenio at night while my father was searching for her. She became paranoid and suspicious that someone was going to poison her. She also began to hear voices telling her to kill herself. She would scream, cursing everybody including her children, as though we were the cause of her illness. When she was out of control my father would call the doctor but all he could do was give her an intravenous shot to put her to sleep. When the medicine wore off she would became unstable again.

One day she started to walk toward the sea. I followed her, trying to persuade her to come back home. Despite my pleading, she kept on going, saying to herself, "I will kill myself by jumping over the cliff into the ocean." I was shocked and terrified. I did not know what to do. I prayed, "Please, Jesus, help me."

She walked up to the cliff while I was crying my heart out. She leaned over the edge of the cliff. I quickly pulled her back by her dress saying to her, "Please Mom, I love you. Please let's go back home. Georgia needs you." I was pleading with her because deep in my heart, I knew that if she jumped, I would go with her and we would both drown.

I yelled, "Mom, please look at me for a minute. I love you and want to help you get well again." I was trying to draw her attention away from the cliff as much as I could. I was stalling her while hoping and praying for a miracle. At that moment, a man walked by and I screamed his way, "Please help me! My mother is going to kill herself by jumping into the ocean!"

He quickly came over, took my mother by the arm, and said to her softly, "I know you are very tired so I will help you by walking you to your home." I was so thankful to God for sending this man to rescue both of us. I thanked him and told him that he was an angel sent by God in a time of great need, saving both of us from death. To this day I continue to believe that this intervention was a miracle.

I was still in shock when I got home. I told my father what happened and he sent for the doctor. The doctor came and gave my mother a shot that made her fall asleep. During this nightmarish time, when our kafenio was closed, we were able to survive for a few weeks with a small savings that my father had from his business. Our neighbors who understood our tragic predicament brought us food from time to time.

A week after the incident at the cliff, my mother went to a vegetable stand and helped herself to apples and pears from the crates, ready to leave without paying for the fruit. The owner saw her and demanded payment, causing my mother to became angry. She dumped the crates of fruit on the sidewalk and ran home.

The owner called the police and a few hours later they came to our home and arrested my mother. I was crying and pleading with them, "Do not take my mom away!" Despite my pleading they shoved her into the back seat of the police car and took her to a mental hospital in Souda near the city of Hania in Crete.

That was the last time I saw my mother. I was only ten years old and from then on my life changed drastically. After the police took my mother away I was filled with grief and sorrow that tore at my heart. My brother Michael was eight and Eleftherios was six years of age. We held each other tightly with tears pouring down our cheeks, mourning the loss of our mother. I was lost and devastated.

I grieved day and night but I had to be strong and learn to take care of my baby sister. Thankfully, the lady next door came to help us and I learned how to make milk formula as well as how to change and wash diapers.

At this point Father's money ran out and we did not have money to buy wood for heat. I was left washing the diapers with cold water. As a result the baby broke out with a severe diaper rash. The rash hurt so much that she could not sleep during the night. My brother Michael and I took turns during the night trying to quiet her down. We had many sleepless nights. Our neighbor came during the day to help care for my sister so that we could get some sleep, but we were still exhausted from being up all night.

1937 was an extremely trying time because of the Depression. My father could not find work in the city, and he left for the village in search of some help. We were left all alone without money with which to buy food. Whenever possible, we would go to the military base and eat the leftovers they gave us.

Father had already obtained a ration card to get canned milk from the Red Cross for the baby. Sometimes we could not get enough milk and I had to dilute the baby's food with water. My sister was getting thinner and thinner. She cried most of the time. There was not enough milk or baby food to keep her alive.

Things got progressively worse. We needed help and we didn't know where to turn. Our struggle to live was becoming hopeless. Then one day, Father came from the village and he brought some bread, olives, and potatoes.

The next day he went to the church to ask for help, leaving us alone with the baby. The baby cried and we all hugged each other, crying for our mother who was not there to take care of us.

When Father came back from talking to the bishop at the church office, he said the Bishop offered to help him. He agreed to write a letter of recommendation to the superintendent of an orphanage located in another town, where my little sister could receive better care. In the letter the Bishop explained the circumstances and the reason for bringing the child there. It was understood that when things got better our sister would come back home to us.

Our neighbor, Toula, the mother of my friends Aleko and Anna, who used to come to our kafenio to enjoy the music, was a big help also. As you may recall, I mentioned that she worked at the orphanage in the outskirts of Iraklion. This is the orphanage where my sister would be taken. From time to time, I would visit Toula and she would be able to tell me how my sister was doing.

We washed our baby sister Georgia's face and put clean clothes on her. We all gathered together with tears pouring down our cheeks once more. We cried as we kissed our baby sister goodbye. As much as we wanted to keep our little sister with us, we could not deny that the orphanage was a better place for her. Father had not found work so he had no money to buy food and he did not know if he would be able to get work soon.

I felt the crushing burden of the disappointments of the last several months since my mother was taken away. I was so young to have lost my beloved mother. I grieved for her for many years and the pain of losing her never went away.

LIFE IN STRANGE HOMES

I now had to face the unexpected challenge of making my own living at ten years of age. I had to find work because my father had no work and no money to buy food. I was very lonely and desolate, but I had no other choice. I prayed to God to help me find the strength and courage to face my new way of life in this world.

My father, brothers, and I did the best we could in the days that followed. One day my father came home from a small gardening job and said, "Aristea, I am not able to find enough work to be able to buy food for you to eat. It is ok for Michael and Eleftherios to go to the military base for food, but because you are a young girl, it is not appropriate for you to go there." Father continued, "Today, when I was working at this couple's home, I told them about our difficult circumstances. They are a young, newlywed couple, and the wife is pregnant. Therefore, she needs some assistance. They offered me to have you come and stay with them in exchange for your help. They are kind people and they have a nice clean home by the sea and you will have food to eat. Until things get better I think it would be good for you to stay there." They had promised my father that they would take good care of me as best they could.

So many thoughts ran through my mind as my father told me this news. I realized that I did not seem to have a choice in the matter. The hurt swelled up inside me all over again. I was worried about what was happening to my mother, I lost my baby sister, and now I had to leave my father and my brothers. To ask a ten-year-old heart to bear this entire trauma and still muster up the courage to move forward was inconceivable. It was like asking an unconscious wounded soldier in the battlefield to bind his own wounds. Despite thinking that I had no more tears to shed, they still welled up in my eyes. I was unable to answer my father, but to myself I said, "If I have to go, then I have to go." I hated to leave my brothers and worried about what would happen to them.

A few days later, in the morning, father told me to gather the few clothes that I had. I put them in my old hand-woven satchel and with the only shoes I owned on my feet, I was ready to leave, but my heart wanted to stay with my brothers. We all cried as I hugged them good-bye and said, "I will come to see you again and I will bring something for you." With that my father and I started down the paved road. The road that we had joyously taken to the sea with our pet pig now seemed dull and fearsome with an unknown life ahead.

When my father and I arrived at the home, Kyria

Zoe greeted us at the door. "Welcome, Kyrios Manoli, please come in." With kindness in her eyes and in her voice, she turned to me and said, "Aristea welcome. We are glad that you have come and we want you to know that you can stay here as long as you like. If at any time you wish to leave, you may." She turned back to my father and said, "Kyrios Manoli you may come back in a few days to see how she is doing." My father turned to me and said, "I will come back and see you soon." Without a hug or a kiss he left.

Kyrios Alekos, her husband, was at work. He had some type of government office job. Kyria Zoe showed me around the beautiful house and finally took me to where my room was. It was a very small room, about the size of a walk-in closet, and it was sparsely decorated with a single bed and a chair. There was nothing on the walls except for a small window that overlooked the garden in the back of the house. They did have a gorgeous view of the Mediterranean Sea.

They permitted me to have most Sundays off, which I spent going back into town to see my brothers who remained at the kafenio. I would also see my friends Aleko and Anna and their mother Toula, who would tell me how Georgia was doing. I was also permitted to continue to go to grade school and I was happy for that.

I slowly became accustomed to my new life, though the aching lingered. Even so, I enjoyed living with Kyrios Alekos and Kyria Zoe and helping them with the housework, as they were very kind to me. They took me to the shoemaker to have new shoes made and the dressmaker to have a couple of new dresses made for me. Kyria Zoe had another lady who would come to cook for large dinner gatherings and make some baked goods like baklava. I was allowed to have some of these treats on special occasions.

Kyrios Alekos had his own study with a small library. I took the liberty of borrowing his detective books, like *Perry Mason*, to read. He had quite a collection so I had the chance to read many books. At that time, I never dreamed that I would someday go to America and see Perry Mason on the television.

Eventually, Kyria Zoe had her baby– a boy named Michael. Fortunately, I was unable to hear him if he cried during the night where I was sleeping. That way I was able to get the rest I needed to be attentive at school. Kyria Zoe took care of him exclusively so that I was exempt from that responsibility.

My father came back a couple of weeks later to see if I was ok. They gave my father a certain amount of money for my services, but I never knew how much. He told me he found another job in a village and that I would not see him again for six months. During one of his visits a year and a half later, he came to see me. It was in the evening and Kyrios Alekos and Kyria Zoe were eating dinner. They invited my father to come in and sit and have something to eat with them. As the 'maid' I would eat my dinner in the kitchen after serving them.

On this particular evening, when they were finished eating they invited me to join them at the table. Kyria Zoe came into the kitchen and said, "Aristea, please come and sit at the table so that you can visit with your father." I came to the table and quietly sat down. I could tell from looking at my father that he seemed sad. I thought he might have lost his job. Instead, he said, "My koumbaro, Mr. Harry, came to see me. He went to visit your mother at the hospital in Souda. When he went they told him that Mother died. He does not know where they buried her." I immediately excused myself and went to my room and sobbed. I prayed to God to please take care of her and rest her soul. Father came to my room a short while later, cracked the door open, and came in. He stood there and said, "Aristea, you know that your mother was very sick and maybe it is best that God came and took her." He then asked me, "How are you getting along here?" I said, "Fine. The people are kind to me and I have a nice place to stay and good food to eat, but I miss my brothers terribly. How are they?"

"Michael went to take a job as a shepherd in the village of Arkalohori and Eleftherios went to live with Yiayia in the village." He paused and then said, "Well, it is getting late now and I have to go. I will come back to see you when I can. Goodnight" I said goodnight and he went out of my room and closed the door. He was gone and I was left by myself to drown in my sorrow.

YIAYIA'S 1939

A month or so after my father's visit, when school was finished for the year, I was homesick and I had to get away from the environment in which I lived. Tired of doing housework and longing to see family, I had a few drachmas and I left Iraklion for Avdou, my Yiayia's village. When I arrived, my yiayia was as happy to see me as I was to see her. My brother, Eleftherios, and my aunt, Athena, were also staying with my grandmother.

It was the end of summer and the grapes were ready for harvesting. People were picking grapes to make wine for home use. Yiayia told us that we could go to work harvesting grapes in the morning. She said that we had to go to bed early after supper and get up early in the morning to go to work. I was so happy to be at Yiayia's that I did not care how much work I had to do.

Yiayia was a generous woman and an excellent cook. There was an old man who lived down the street, and every time my Yiayia cooked something special she would make me take a plateful to the poor man. She would always take in strangers and share a little food with them. It was not unusual for a poor person traveling on foot to go door to door to see who might give them something to eat. They would knock and say, "Offer an act of mercy?"

Every evening, the table was set and we all waited for Yiayia to sit down. We then made the sign of the cross and thanked God for the food. My Yiayia used to say that greed and ingratitude were the worst faults. She was very religious and invoked God in her everyday decisions. We had very little but we were happy.

The next day, to my surprise, my father came. He was so happy to see all of us. He wanted to help my yiayia harvest the grapes. We got up early and worked like beavers all day. Yiayia was happy to have us help her. We brought all the grapes in so that my father could get them ready to crush. We crushed the grapes the next day. Father emptied the buckets of juice into barrels where it would become wine.

I had a great time that summer and fall at my yiayia's. You see, during this time, good things were few, and we thanked the Lord for our daily bread, unlike today when dogs are fed instead of humans and nobody dreams of saying thank you.

One thing I remember about my Yiayia was that she taught me to have a deep devotion to God, which has given me great strength, courage, and the determination to endure all the hardships I was going through then, as well as those I would endure in the future. I learned that when I face difficult situations that I am unable to solve on my own, I just need to pray to God for his help.

LEAVING YIAYIA'S

Several weeks had passed since we harvested the grapes. The summer was over and the autumn air smelled like rain. It was nearly the end of August and it was time to leave my Yiayia's home. While we were eating breakfast, I explained that I wanted to stay longer, but that I must leave Saturday for Iraklion so that I could go to school.

Yiayia explained, "My dear child, I know education is very important now, especially for girls. When I was a young child, it was thought that only men must be educated. I had to help my parents on the farm and also help with the housework. I am saddened that I never learned to read or write.

Saturday came and my yiayia accompanied me to the bus stop. Yiayia gave me a big hug and said, "God be with you." I got on the bus and waived my hand good-bye as the tears rolled toward my mouth and I could taste the salt from them. As the bus took off, I screamed, "I'll see you next summer!"

Aunt Kaliope was expecting me and was at the bus stop waiting for me when I arrived. Aunt Kaliope was my mother's first cousin, however, to show her respect I called her *Aunt*. She was tall and slim with beautiful dark eyes and she always had a big smile on her face. She gave me a warm greeting and said, "We will walk to the house. It is only a few blocks away."

When we got to the house, she cooked spaghetti and baked homemade bread. She had two children, a daughter named Marika and a son named Kyriakos. Marika was two years younger than me, and Kyriakos was three years younger than her. Aunt Kaliope became a widow at a very young age. I do not recall what her husband died from. She worked at a hospital for the elderly to make a living for her children.

After school, Marika would go to a special program to learn how to make custom clothing for women. After four years of study, she received a diploma that gave her the credibility needed to open her own business. She was an excellent designer and seamstress. Eventually she moved to Athens where she opened her own shop and became well known by wealthy woman. She acquired a good clientele and made an excellent living.

Marika's brother Kyriakos joined the merchant marines at a very young age. He always loved the sea and made this his career for life. He toured many countries. One of his trips took him to San Diego in 1964. I was already in America at that time and my family went to meet him. We were so happy to see him after so many years. We were together for a couple of days and he showed us the big ship. He had come via Japan to load the ship with scrap iron and take it back. It was a pleasure to see Kyriakos. We had a great time together and we took him on a tour of San Diego. We had dinner in a nice restaurant. It was an unforgettable time. Every time we speak on the phone he talks about it.

I was so grateful to Theia Kaliope for extending to me her hospitality and allowing me to stay with her while I tried to continue my school education. The company of my cousins was such a comfort to me since my mother died and I was separated from my father and brothers. Times were difficult and Theia Kaliope worked very hard at the nursing home in order to try to save money to send Marika to the clothing design school. While she never said anything and she shared whatever she had, I recognized how difficult things were. Not wanting to be an extra burden to her I decided that once school was over I would find a place to work during the summer months that I would be out of school.

My cousins and I enjoyed the summer of 1940 together. We did whatever work we could while Theia Kaliope was at work at the seniors' home. When we could, we enjoyed going to the plaza in town. During the summer we would go and sit on top of the Venitian walls around Iraklion and look down at the gardens where they would play movies on a large screen. It was the only way for Marika, Kyriakos, and I to watch movies, as we had no money to pay to enter the theater. Sometimes there would be stage shows such as acrobatics or musicals. Those days were very special.

One summer morning my Theia had a surprise
visitor from a village. I did not know from which village he
came and I can't remember who he was. I believe that he
was a relative of her deceased husband. He was invited in
for breakfast. My cousins were not at home. I was invited
to sit at the table with them while they talked about life and
caught up on the news since the last time they had seen
each other. In the middle of the conversation this
unexpected visitor casually said to Theia, "Did you hear the
news about Kyrios Manoli?"

"No", she replied, "Tell me."

"Well, I bumped into him at the kafenio in Partera. I
asked him how he was doing and he said that he had just
got married to a woman from Vasiliki" It was said matter-
of-factly, as if he was reporting that watermelons had gone
up in price. Theia was surprised but graceful, as she simply
replied, "Oh, really?" I myself was shocked! I was still
grieving from the death of my mother two years before.
Now to hear that my father went and married another
woman, a complete stranger, was like pouring lemon juice
on a fresh cut. That I was to have a stepmother who would
invade my life was too much for me to bear at that
moment. I quickly excused myself and went outside to cry
my heart out once again! Niagra Falls could not compete
with my tears.

A short while later, my Theia came out with the
visitor and bid him goodbye. Theia Kaliope saw me crying
and she beckoned me in, "Come in Aristea, let us talk."
Theia Kaliope tried her best to console my broken heart.

"Please listen to me. Your father is still very young and he is in need of companionship, therefore he has chosen to marry. You do not need to worry too much. You are at the age now where you are old enough to make your own living so you will not have to live with them. You will only see them occasionally." Her consolation was like putting a Band-Aid on an amputated leg. This news destroyed any hope of ever being together as family as we had known it.

In September of 1940 I took a job working for an attorney and his wife. The attorney, Mr. Kounelakis, and his wife, Nista, had two children, Manoli and Eleni. Eleni was nineteen and her brother, Manoli was fourteen, the same age as I was. Kyria Nitsa was deaf and she needed help when company came to her home, as she could not hear the doorbell ringing or the mailman bringing the mail. Grocery shopping and other household errands were also to be my responsibility. The one thing that I was grateful for was that this job was only one mile from Theia Kaliope and my cousins. I hated being held captive as a maid, but for the time being the luxuriant home of the attorney was extremely comfortable. It was welcoming to be in such a nice environment where I could have my own room with a clean bed, clothes, and good food to eat. Sundays I would be off duty unless they were to have company for a Sunday dinner. I would use these days to see Theia Kaliope, Marika and Kyriakos.

Aunt Kaliope and I in 1943 in Iraklion

Me at 17 and my Cousin Marika, 15.

WORLD WAR II

I had been working for Mr. Kounelakis and his family for barely two months before we heard the news that war had come to Greece's northwestern borders. I could not help but remember the simple exchange that my father had had with the military men who used to visit our kafenio regarding the possibility of war.

It was October when the German ally and fascist dictator of Italy, Benito Mussolini, issued an ultimatum to the Greek government to either allow Italy to freely enter Greece through the Albanian mountains or there would be war. Greece was given three hours to respond, as the Italian military was already positioned in Albania, ready to enter at Greece. The Prime Minister of Greece, Ioannis Metaxas replied unequivocally to the Italians, *OXI!*, which in English simply means *NO!* The Italians outnumbered the Greeks and were fortified with tanks that the Greek army did not possess. It is said that any practical leader would have recognized this and submitted to the Italians. Nevertheless, the Greeks went to war and the country was behind Metaxas.

The Greek army fought aggressively in the rugged mountains of Albania. During the six months of fighting against Italians, the brave Greek army successfully won many victories. Each victory was celebrated in Iraklion with the city band playing the national anthem while school children marched down the avenues waving small Greek flags.

The church bells rang throughout Greece as the radio announcer blasted out the news of our military victories. People flocked the streets. They were delirious with joy as they celebrated the miraculous events. They were so proud, grateful, and inspired by the heroic example that the Greek military men had demonstrated while fighting on the rugged mountains of Albania. Unfortunately, a black cloud appeared over the horizon and our joyful victory didn't last long. As the Greek military was winning the war against the Italians, the Germans were taking European nations over one at a time.

When the Germans saw Greek army's victory over the Italians, they initiated their own invasion of Greece via Yugoslavia. The Germans captured many Greek military men. They placed them in camps surrounded by barbed wire and thousands of them perished from sickness and starvation. Despite the tremendous odds against them, the Greek men had fought with an unbreakable spirit and had succeeded in winning the first Allied land victory of World War Two. This was not a small accomplishment, as the Greek victory delayed Hitler's invasion of the Soviet Union

until the brutal winter months, when the Germans had to
fight the winter as much as anything else. Winston
Churchill is quoted as saying of the Greek people, "From
hence forth we shall not say that Greeks fight like heroes,
but that heroes fight like Greeks."

With the German invasion of Greece, transportation
was disrupted and farmers were unable to deliver food.
Many people in Athens starved to death. There was a
newspaper report that people were digging into garbage
containers for food. When they could not find any food,
they killed rats to eat. The survival circumstances were very
bleak for the Athenian people.

It was about the end of April 1941 when my father
came from Vitsilia, the village where he lived with his new
wife, to see me at Mr. Kounelakis' home. My father
reported to me that my brother, Michael, was still sheep
herding in Arkalohori and that Eleftherios was still living
with Yiayia.

My father came to get me to return with him to
Vasiliki. He said, "I was told the Germans will invade Crete
soon and I want you to come with me to Pitslilia where I
know you will be safe." Although, I did not want to go to
live with my stepmother, it once again looked like I did not
have a choice.

I finally accepted the fact that I had to go with my
father to the village to be safe. I packed my suitcase, bid the
family that I worked for goodbye, and with tears in my eyes
we departed. When we went to the square to take the bus,
we discovered that the drivers were on strike so we walked

the thirty-five kilometers to the village.

On the way, we met a farmer who was going in the same direction and he offered to load my suitcase onto his mule. I was grateful for his help. I began to feel very tired on the way, so we stopped in a village where my father knew a family friend. As we approached his home, we saw his friend, John, giving water to his donkey. When John saw my father he immediately embraced him and invited us into his home. My father explained to him that we walked all day, as the buses were on strike. John's wife, Ekaterini, was very friendly. "Have a seat," she said. "You must be exhausted from walking all day. Stay and join us for dinner. It will be ready shortly."

We enjoyed the dinner and the company. My father and John listened to the news on the radio and discussed the war. The radio that said that the Germans were planning to invade Crete soon, and Father and John were concerned about what might happen. Ekaterini suggested that we should stay and rest overnight in their home. This way we could be refreshed for our journey the next morning. Father and I were so tired that we gratefully accepted the invitation.

The next morning, Ekaterini prepared a fresh, homemade breakfast of bread, cheese, and tea. After we finished breakfast we thanked them for their hospitality and said goodbye. Father invited them to come and visit us in Vitsilia.

We began to walk toward the village. Farther down the road we met a couple that was going in the same direction to another village. Father asked if they would help us with our suitcase. They were glad to help and the man tied the suitcase on his donkey right away. They said that they were from Iraklion. They also left their home, afraid to face the impending German invasion. Their parents were excitedly waiting for them in a village past Vitsilia.

Vitsilia is a village located on a high plateau. The only way to get there was by donkey or by walking up a twisting, rocky trail. My Father, speaking as we walked along, told us that the soil was very fertile there: vineyards thrived and produced good wine. Also, olive groves grew in abundance despite water being scarce. If rain was not plentiful in the winter season, the orchards might suffer from drought.

We walked the rocky path up, down, and around the hills. The soles of my shoes were torn apart, so I had to walk barefoot. I was exhausted and my toes were bleeding. It seemed like forever, but late in the evening we finally saw signs of the village. As we approached, I noticed the homes were in broken fragments.

I asked my father, "Where are the people?" He said that the Turks dynamited the homes before they left the village in 1912. Fortunately, some residents survived the blast. About twelve families lived among the ruins.

At last we entered the home of my father and his new wife, Vasiliki. It was a one-room windowless house made of stone. There was a raised stone platform that was two feet higher than the rest of the room. My father and stepmother slept there. Since there was no bed for me to sleep on, my father threw me a blanket and I collapsed on the earthen floor.

LIFE IN VITSILIA

The morning after we arrived in Vitsilia, Father was anxious and proud to show me his vegetable garden. He already had lettuce, fava beans, and artichokes growing. Then we walked among some ruins, I noticed a structure that looked different from the others. We stepped inside and Father said that this was a church called St. George. I saw frescoes on the wall that looked as fresh as the day they had been painted. It was a beautiful church, but now the roof was falling in and the colorful stained glass windows were broken. Only part of the stone sanctuary remained. Many such ruins littered the village of Vitsilia.

My father told me of a project he was doing. He was tearing down the abandoned ruins stone by stone and building retaining walls along the perimeter of what would become the garden. He placed the largest stones on the outside and then filled the center with the smaller stones. The cleared area would provide the room needed for a summer vegetable garden. My job was to fill the gaps of the wall with small rocks. Father filled a pail with rocks and I emptied it into the wall until it was full. This was my job for the rest of the summer along with other chores.

The introduction of my stepmother into my life showed me that she was not keen about my presence at her palace. Her reception was cool and I felt quite unwelcome. She seemed unable to relate to me as a mother in any capacity. Vasiliki's widowed mother lived behind us on the next block with her two other daughters and a son. She also had another son but he lived far away in Athens. Vasiliki's younger sister was the first person to be enlisted in investigating the newcomer from Iraklion, the city girl. I eventually met the whole family. Her sisters treated me well and her brother, who was sixteen, was very kind to me.

That summer I developed a friendship that I never anticipated. It was a warm relationship, unlike the one I had with my stepmother. My new friend was my father's goat. She was a young goat and took a liking to me to the point that she followed me wherever I went. I would hide in the vineyards and she would come to find me. It was like playing a game. At night she would come inside the house with me. When it was time for bed (I finally had a bed that I made by putting sagebrush under my blanket) I would lay down and the goat would kiss my face by licking me. Then it would lie down next to me and sleep. As soon as I got up, she popped right up to join me.

While my father and I were tearing down the walls of the ruins and building the walls for the garden, something wonderful took place. We discovered a beautiful view of the valley that was below. Some weeks passed and it was now the end of April, time to plant the summer season vegetables such as watermelon, zucchini, and squash. The food from the garden would not only help to sustain us, but also enable us to share some with the other villagers.

There was an artesian well at the bottom of a steep hill below the garden. That summer, when I was fifteen, I had to make many trips up and down the rocky trail to bring enough water to maintain the vegetable garden. Some days it was over a hundred degrees. For that reason, I had to get up at five in the morning to make sure that I carried enough water before the sun got too hot. I had no shoes and the stones on the path were very hot to walk on. It would take me four hours to go up and down this rocky path. Many times I would bump my toes on the sharp stones, which made my feet bleed. My toes were bandaged all summer long.

Once, when I went down to the well, I met a girl named Angela. She was the same age as me and lived with her family near my father's property. We talked a lot and from then on became close friends. At the end of our day's work she would often invite me to her house for lunch.

One morning at the well, I met a teenager who said he was herding his sheep there, because the grass grew greener near the well and the sheep had plenty of water to drink there. His name was John. He said, "You don't look like anyone from this area. Where are you from?"

"I am from Iraklion. I came to avoid the German invasion of the city," I replied.

That same day, John's friend, Christo, came along with

his sheep. John, who had never been to the city, was eager to learn what it was like to live there. I described the electric lights, stores decorated with colorful neon signs, and museums that contained archeological exhibits. I told him about movie theaters and the city band that played in the park every Sunday. John was overwhelmed. He said, "I wish that someday I could travel there and experience the modern life of the city."

As the days went by, word spread around the village that a young girl from Iraklion was in town and that she knew all about the city life. "You ought to hear her talk," they would say. As time went on, I met more and more of the teenagers from the area and about half a dozen boys popped up like mushrooms.

I became very popular that summer – the central attraction. In the conversations we had, the boys expressed how much they enjoyed talking to me and how much they admired my superior vocabulary and knowledge. John said, "You speak the educated language. We are villagers and we don't know very much, that is why we like to hear you talk. We learn so much just by listening to you speak your educated language."

A week went by and John did not come to the well. I asked Angela, my new friend, if she heard anything about him. She said, "No, I have not heard anything either." Then, one day at the well, we met John's friend Christo. He said, "He had a fight with his father and they threw chairs at each other. One chair landed on John's foot and broke his toe."

Christo had been there, and heard John's father say, "Ever since you met that girl from Iraklion you got brainwashed and you don't have your mind on your work. If you go to see her again I'll break your other foot so that you will not be able to go anywhere." Two weeks later, John came to the well with Christo. He brought some homemade bread and cheese to share with us. He said that one of the other boys had told his father that we were meeting alone, which was not true. "However," he said, "No matter what my father says, he cannot stop me from coming here to talk with you." We all continued our friendship and conversation throughout the summer.

Besides meeting at the well, we had another customary meeting place on Sundays. About a mile away was a group of oak trees. This spot become an important place on our Sunday afternoons. Usually, on Sunday afternoons, the group of boys from the well would come to the field to let their animals graze. While they were there, they would climb the oak trees and sit on the branches like monkeys.

They could see Angela and I across the field, sitting on the wall that my father had built. They would scream, whistle, holler, wave their hands, and carry on for hours. They would yell to us, "Come and join us. We want you to speak to us so we can hear more about Iraklion. We like to listen to you speak." Of course, Angela would wave back and urge them on. Vasiliki's younger sisters would join us on the wall.

This performance went on practically every Sunday. We looked forward to their attention, as it was the only fun we had in the small village. However, my stepmother would get very angry. She would say, "Since you arrived there is no peace in the village. You have turned the entire area upside down. Your father never told me he had other children!"

After my arrival to Vitsilia, it didn't take long until Vasiliki started trying to keep me busy by shouting out orders, "Go pick clover to feed the goat. Go gather some dandelion greens for dinner. Stop wasting time doing nothing and go fetch some water." The truth is, I realized she began to show the signs of pregnancy soon after I got there. In retrospect, I can see how she must have been extremely pressured with an unexpected stepdaughter, the threat of war, and a pregnancy. Even so, her unkindness toward me became progressively worse.

One thing was for certain: she seemed to resent me because my command of the Greek language reflected my education, which was superior to hers. She also disliked the kindness that her sixteen-year-old brother extended to me by bringing me gifts of *paximathi* (dry toasted bread). As far as I was concerned, Vitsilia was a peaceful place to live regardless of my stepmother's claims that my arrival made it otherwise.

An interesting thing I learned and observed in the summer of 1941 was rope making. My father was busy making rope all that summer. There was a special cactus plant that grew near the village olive grove. This kind of cactus has long, sharp, sword-like leaves with spiky thorns. Father cut the leaves and laid them in the sun to dry for several days. Then he stripped the dry part from the leaves. He combed the leaf so that all the fibers lay one way. This allowed him to twist the fibers into yarn. He combined several yarns to make a single, long strand, and then combined as many strands as necessary to make a strong rope. Using this process, it took my father about two months to make several lengths of strong rope, which was primarily used by the villagers to secure their animals when they grazed in the meadows. Father's rope was also used for making baskets. When the rope making process was complete, Father loaded the ropes onto the donkey and took them to the town bazaar to trade for other things we needed. He did this in between other jobs that occupied his time.

There was another important project that he undertook. A few months after my arrival, folks coming from other villages told him that the Germans were driving up in their trucks and confiscating whatever the people had – olive oil, wheat, potatoes, beans, and anything else they desired. Upon hearing this, father dug a deep pit at one edge of the garden to store anything the Germans might try to take. He lined the bottom of the pit with straw and then alternated layers of potatoes, carrots, and other vegetables, with more straw in between to keep the produce fresh. He placed metal containers of olive oil on top and then covered the rest of the pit with straw. He finished by placing old boards and rocks on top of the pit so that if the Germans came looking for food they would not notice anything.

Perhaps the most important project Father undertook that summer was the building of a bomb shelter. Father, along with two other men from the village, excavated a tunnel into the side of a hill; it was thirty feet long and four feet in circumference. At the end of the tunnel they discovered an old, dry well. Upon finding this, they built a wooden ladder, which could be used as an escape route up to the top of the well, in case the front of the tunnel was blocked by an explosion.

All of us were terrified and afraid that the Germans would come and bomb our village. We slept outdoors in bamboo shacks with the mosquitos eating us alive. We all wondered what would happen to us if the Germans occupied Crete and we were all frightened. I remembered my father saying, "I fought one war already and I was a prisoner for ten months in Turkey, but I never thought I would have to fight on my own peaceful island. I don't know what the future will bring but if I have to defend my country once more, I will."

As the summer went on, things were heating up in my stepmother's house and I had my own explosions to contend with. I was assaulted with continual complaints and verbal abuse. My stepmother told me that she wished to see me as a prostitute on the street. She said words that pierced my heart like a sword. Angela realized that my stepmother resented me, and her mother, who was aware of the situation, would try to make my life more pleasant by inviting me to her house for lunch and consoling me. She was very kind and compassionate.

Then one quiet afternoon, our peacefulness was broken by a tremendous sound. We realized that a fleet of airplanes was flying overhead. Everyone bolted from their homes yelling and screaming, "Run to the tunnel! The Germans are coming!" We all were so scared that we dashed for the tunnel. A ninety-year-old lady wanted to get to the tunnel ahead of us and slowed the rest of us down. The German airplanes began bombing us at the same time as machine gun shells rained over us.

The old lady moved so slowly that we did not have time to get into the tunnel as the bombs were coming nearer to us. They exploded around us and sent rocks and dirt everywhere. We could see trees being uprooted in the distance. We almost got killed. We had to run pass the old lady to get into the tunnel. Just as we almost reached the entrance, one of the bombs exploded right in front of the tunnel and made a big hole. We were very lucky that it barely missed us. Miraculously, in all of that bombing no one got hurt, thanks be to God. But for the first time the war was no longer a story far away, frequent air raids became a routine part of our lives. Sometimes we all had to run to the shelter as often as three times in one day. During these frightening times, everyone would remain huddled in the tunnel, keeping the children quiet. When we grew hungry, one brave woman at a time would go back to the houses to prepare food for us all.

For days we all watched the bombing. I was fifteen years old and horrified and frightened like the rest of the people in the village. My father was a leader in the village.

Everyone respected him and looked to him for advice. He was a fighter. The entire village admired his patriotism and his knowledge and experience earlier wars. He was the protector and advisor of the village. I was proud of the achievements and industriousness of my father. The memories of this time spent with my father are etched permanently in my mind.

A week after the first bombing, we saw in the distance a line of German military trucks coming toward the village. We were all terrified. The old lady was brave. She said, "You all run for the tunnel. I'll stay here behind the door with a crowbar in my hand. I'll be ready for the first one who peaks through the door. As they come in, I will crack them behind the neck with the crowbar and they will hit the ground one at a time." We all laughed at her bravery and dashed for the tunnel.

Two hours later, she came to the tunnel and told us the German soldiers never came where she was hiding. She said they made a lot of noise shooting their guns in the air. However, in the end they did not find anything except two chickens in the chicken coup. They took the chickens, turned around, and left.

Peace in the village became sporadic, as did any peace in my heart and soul and in my stepmother's house. Things were becoming unbearable and I decided to write a letter to my Theia Kaliope in Iraklion. My letter was short.

Dear Theia,
I believe that I have spent enough time here and I prefer to

return to Iraklion. I would like to know if I could come and
stay with you until I find work.
Love,
Aristea

As I waited for her response, the days felt like forever.
In the meantime, one day, a bomb went off in the house,
not literally. My stepmother went digging through my
personal belongings and found some personal letters. She
did not know how to read, so she employed a neighbor to
come and read it to her. I was not at home, but Angela had
come looking for me and found them in the middle of
reading my letters. Angela came to find me and told me
what had happened. Of course I was furious at this
violation of the few personal belongings I had. I decided
not to say anything, believing that I would soon leave. I did
not want to have any more confrontations or hear her
vicious, stinging remarks.

I did everything I could to please my stepmother.
However, she did not appreciate anything I did for her. She
always complained. You could not imagine how heartless
she was when my father was not around. Many times, I
hesitated to stay alone with her, as I was afraid that if she
got really angry she might throw hot water at me and burn
my face.

About one week later, the letter carrier came back to
tell me that my Theia said I was welcome to come anytime.
I was so relieved to hear the good news. I decided I would
wait until September to return to Iraklion. Unfortunately,

there was another incident. My father took sides with my stepmother and I had enough. I decided to leave a few days later around the end of August. I left unannounced and therefore did not have a chance to say good-bye to Angela. Instead of going directly to Iraklion, I went to Arkalohori to see my brother, Michael. I thought to myself that I would go there to try to find work and make enough money to pay my way to Iraklion.

Arkalohori was a commercial village and I had gone there with my father when he went to sell his ropes. I had not seen Michael, then because he was out in the hills herding the sheep. I had sent word ahead to him that I would be coming in a few days. It had been a few years since I had seen him. He anticipated my arrival and I went to find him at the home in which he was staying at the outskirts of town.

I knocked on the door and when the lady of the house opened it, I said, "Hi, I'm Aristea, Michael's sister. I came to see my brother." She said, "Yes, come in. Michael told us that you would be coming." After Michael came out to greet me, we went outside so that we could talk freely together. We both cried our eyes out and poured out our hearts to one another. I could see that he was not doing well. He said, "I miss you. The winters here are so severe that my clothes do not keep me warm. I tried to put a blanket over myself but it is not enough." He looked very thin and it was evident that he was not eating well. I told him that I missed him and found a job there for a little while, so that I could then see him more often. I told him I was working at the house of a family who needed me to look after their small boy. I told him where the house was so that he could come see me when he was able. We were both happy that we were going to see each other for a while. When he did come to visit, I gave him part of my food that I saved for him.

By the time I departed for Iraklion, a few months later, the German army had occupied all the major cities on Crete. It was a sad parting with Michael. I told him that I would try to look for work for him in the city, and if I found something I would write to let him know. That gave him and I a little hope that maybe the two of us could be closer together. With that, I departed on the bus for Iraklion.

THE BATTLE OF CRETE

Crete is in a strategic location in the Mediterranean as it lies between three continents: Europe to the north, Asia to the east and Africa to the south. Because of this strategic location, Crete was very important to the Germany military.

The British Allied Forces were granted permission from the Greek government to use its airfields located on the northern coast of the island. The Germans were fearful that the British would use the airfields on the northern coast to bomb the Plaosti oil fields in Romania. This would be a devastating to the German war effort.

Romania was allied with Germany in the Second World War and gave the Germans permission to use their oil fields to power German airplanes, submarine ships, trucks and tanks, which were necessary to continue the German war effort.

In May 1941 the Germans invaded Crete. The first division arrived in Hania, the capital of Crete. They came with gliders that carried the paratroopers. Most of the people of Crete had never seen a parachute and when they saw German military men dropping from the sky, they thought they were devils coming from another planet.

"These devils are invading our beautiful island. This must be the end of the world," they cried. The Cretans fought fiercely. It was an indescribable feat of heroism and perseverance in the face of such deadly opposition.

The first group of nine gliders invaded Hania, Crete. Three crashed against the rocky hills. Most paratroopers were killed before they hit the ground. Paratroopers continued to come down from the sky by the hundreds. At the same time, German airplanes were dropping bombs over the city. They sky became black from the smoke and we could see the red flames burst toward the sky from the hill of Vitsilia. The city of Hania, according to the news report, was like hell on Earth.

Men, woman and children fought the enemy as they landed down on the ground. The Cretans fought with clubs, shovels and crowbars. They would take the dead paratroopers guns to shoot the others as they were descending toward the battlefield. Some of the paratroopers who landed on the olive trees did not make it to the ground. The Cretans who were hiding under the trees gunned them down before the paratroopers had a chance to jump safely down from the trees.

The first day of the battle in Hania very few paratroopers survived. The battle continued and casualties were heavy. The first day was a great victory for the Cretan men and woman who fought the Germans. Hundreds of the German paratroopers lay dead and wounded. The

German timetable for the invasion of Rethimnon was running out of time. The goal of capturing the airfield of the eastern side of Rethimnon was 1:00 pm and it was rapidly approaching. It was just the beginning of the death and bloodshed.

The German military forces were comprised of 2,900 men. They were well equipped with heavy machine guns, mortars and airborne artillery. The military force of the Australians and Cretans were outnumbered in manpower and equipment. But lieutenant Campbell, the had commander of the Australian and the Cretan battalion, was determined to defend the airfield located five miles east of the city of Rethimnon. All Campbell had with which to stop the German attack were two Australian battalions made up of 600 men and four Cretan battalions made up of 1,200 men. The Australian men were poorly trained and equipped and the regiments had only four anti aircraft guns, one 100-MM cannon and four 75-MM French field pieces.

The artillery pieces had no sights for aiming and only 80 shells for the three-inch mortars. The men lacked grenades and they were short of rifle ammunition. Of the Cretan men, many had no rifles and those who did had only ten bullets per weapon.

Campbell split the men in three divisions. He positioned them in strategic hiding locations so as not to be seen by enemy airplanes. With his battalions well entrenched in their defensive positions, Campbell sat back and waited for the German onslaught. At 4:00 pm they bomber airplanes finally made their appearance over the Rethimnon area.

No sooner had they made their appearance than the Cretans and the Australians opened fire. One of the airplanes tried to avoid ground fire and sliced into another just as they were releasing the paratroopers. The planes both broke into pieces and drowned at sea- all the men perished. Another transport caught fire and turned back out to sea trailing with smoke.

The battle lasted over three hours. At least 1,000 paratroopers were killed. It proved that the Cretans and Australians were victorious that night. The loss of life was great on both sides. However, the fight continued.

The enemy poured in fresh troops by the thousands. The British, New Zealanders, and the Australians fought side by side with the Cretans. They mowed the German paratroopers down as they descended. It was an indescribable feat of heroism and perseverance in the face of such deadly opposition.

Unfortunately the Allies ran out of ammunition and were forced to retreat into the mountains before the Germans took Crete. At last the Germans occupied Crete, but the war there never ended. Cretan military men continued to hide up in the mountains and fought the Germans by destroying airplanes, burning military supplies and blowing up German tanks and trucks. Most of the allies, with the help of the Cretans, escaped by the southern side of the island as British ships waited on near the shore to rescue them.

After the massacre of the German paratroopers, Hitler discontinued this type of operation. Crete became known as the graveyard of the German paratroopers.

THE BRITISH ON THE MOUNTAINS OF CRETE 1941

On June first 1941, after the German occupation of Crete, the farming people had a difficult time with the German Military police. The Germans would go to the villages and search our homes for food. Without permission, they would load trucks with whatever they could find - olive oil, potatoes, beans, onions, and flour. Even homemade blankets were taken. Farmers, fearing deportation to labor camps, left their fields and headed for the mountains. Women and children were left to plow the land, plant wheat, beans, and other vegetables in order to feed their families. The women also supplied food for the men on the mountains.

It did not take long for the Cretan men living in the ragged mountains to become well organized. In fact, some of the British, Australian, and New Zealander officers soon joined them there. The British were able to communicate with the Cairo Secret Intelligence Service, keeping the men informed about the outcome of the war on the front lines.

The German Military Police became very angry from this embarrassing situation. They soon posted a notice in various public buildings proclaiming that for every German soldier killed, they would line up ten civilians and shoot them on the spot. Although the people became terrified upon hearing the news, the continuation of guerrilla warfare against the Germans never stopped.

The first year of the occupation there was an ordinance that no civilians were permitted to be on the streets after eight o'clock. If the German police found anyone outdoors they would be arrested and put in prison. They even deported Greek citizens to Germany to work in their factories. If anyone were not able to work because of sickness, they would not hesitate to shoot them.

A Special Air Service team was sent from Africa for special missions to Crete. One night in early spring, coming from the south side of the island, they succeeded in entering the airport in Iraklion by cutting the barbed wire and then placing explosives on twenty Junger - 88S, German bombers. The explosives were detonated at midnight and the force was so great that the whole city shook. The noise could be heard everywhere. Most of the people believed it to be an earthquake.

All of a sudden we saw flames shooting up into the sky from the airport and knew then that someone started the fire. The next day we heard from the people who lived near the airport that the airplanes burned all night. The Germans reported on the radio that most of the bombers were destroyed. The group from Africa escaped the south shore of Crete before the Germans discovered the damage. One of the guerrillas who helped them escape said the British boasted joyfully for their success in destroying the German bombers. However, the next day the Germans executed fifty Cretan men, including Mr. Tito Georgiathis, who was both the Governor of Crete and a seventy-year-old priest.

The Cretans blamed the British for the execution of the men. However, hatred toward the British did not last long as the British supplied the Cretan guerillas in the mountains with guns and ammunitions to use against the Germans. British brought supplies by submarine, notifying the guerrillas of their arrival so they could help unload and carry the munitions up the mountains to their camp.

MY RETURN TO IRAKLION

When the bus departed from Arkalohori, I became uneasy about what I would find ahead. There were no German soldiers in Arkalohori at this time. The bus driver had announced before our departure that they had permission to transport people, but there would be bus inspections at various stops. He said, "Unless you are carrying weapons or are involved with the resistance you have no need to worry. When they inspect the bus they are only looking for guns or people involved with the resistance. So far, we have not had any problems, so do not panic when we stop."

It was scary for me to not know what I would find in Iraklion. As we traveled, I began to see German soldiers and army trucks with swastikas on the side. When we made our first stop, a German soldier came on the bus to walk up and down the aisle. I was very nervous despite what the bus driver had said. At that time, a person did not know if they were going to get arrested for an unknown reason.

When I returned to Iraklion to stay with my Aunt, I

discovered that the German occupation had changed the way of life for people in the city. Nothing was the same. After the invasion, the Germans had taken over wealthy families' homes. They took their furniture, china, crystal, and silver and shipped the precious goods to Germany. I found out that German officers occupied the home of Mr. Kounelakis, the attorney whom I had worked for, and that he and his family were forced to rent a small apartment.

People went hungry during the German occupation. The stores were empty and everything was closed. Business people had moved out of the city before the Germans came. Some moved to the villages with their relatives, and those without relatives made their homes under the olive trees.

When it was safe, peasants brought produce to sell in the market. However, they would not accept money. Only tangible items of real value, such as gold and silver, could be exchanged for goods. After a couple of months a black market emerged. Women that had gold rings, bracelets, and necklaces sold them to purchase flour and olive oil at the exorbitantly inflated prices of the black market. One bakery that was still open for business wanted fifteen million drachmas for a single loaf of bread. It took a whole wheelbarrow of money to buy this single item. A month later, the money became worthless and could be seen flying all over the streets.

Many men, women, and children would go hungry every night, suffering from malnutrition. People with typhoid, cholera, and whooping cough surrounded us.

Many of the sick people died daily. We were hungry and cold, as there was no money to buy wood for the fire. We were constantly afraid the bombings would kill us. There seemed to be no way of ridding ourselves of the fear that something tragic was about to happen.

Finally, after months of hunger, sickness, and misery, the Red Cross came and distributed seven pounds of flour and a bag of dehydrated potatoes to each family. The delivery came once each month and was free of charge. In the meantime, English airplanes were bombing the Germans, but sometimes missed the bases and bombed the cities instead.

My aunt, cousins, and I had to run to the shelter under the school building and stay there until the alarm sounded. Sometimes we would run to the shelter three times in a single day. At times we did not even have time to eat our dinner. Our food would be served and the air raid siren would sound. Our food would be left on the table as we ran for the shelter. It seemed that we lived through this scenario a thousand times.

One afternoon, Aunt Kaliope gave me a letter to deliver to a friend of hers. Evidently the mailman left it at our house by mistake. On my way back home, the English air bombers came by surprise. They were targeting the military base but accidentally bombed the suburbs. The bombs began dropping like rain. Without time to make it to the shelter, I dove into a ditch on the side of the road. Terrified, I said my prayers, thinking that this would be the last hour of my life on this earth. I lay there motionless while the bombs buzzed over me. One of the bombs exploded so near that the sound of the impact hurt my ears, which didn't recover for a full month. My body was covered with rocks and dirt. I lay there in shock for what seemed like hours. I heard a man asking if I needed help. He came over and took the rocks off my body and lifted me up. I had a few bruises, but, thank God, I was lucky to escape with my life. On the way home I saw the devastation the bombs had caused. I saw the crushed buildings and was struck with the sad realization that there were crushed people under those buildings. So many terrible things happened in those years and the memories are imprinted in my brain forever.

Even though the Germans invaded our lives, I knew I had to keep going. Mrs. Kounelakis' sister lived close to my theia and saw me together with my theia. She mentioned that her sister was looking for assistance, but that they had moved into an apartment. I told her, "Well, I just came back from the village and I would like to go back to work." She answered, "I will let them know."

A few days later I saw her again and she conveyed to me that they would like me to come and work for them. Saturday morning, after breakfast, I walked to their home. Mr. Kounelakis greeted me warmly, "Hi Aristea, come in. It's good to see you. So you just came from the village and are looking to work again?"

"Yes," I replied.

"Well, you can come here whenever you are ready and you may bring your clothes with you." With that, a few days later, I said good-bye to Theia Kaliope, Marika, and Kyriakos and started working again at the Kounelakis' new apartment.

I felt sorry for them that they were forced to give up their old home and move to the apartment. They had to leave all of their furniture and many of their possessions behind. Their apartment was simply furnished. I did not have my own room here, but instead, I slept on a couch in the hallway. Down the hall there was a very small armoire into which I could put my clothes and belongings. I was so happy to be away from Pitslilia, even if the Germans occupied the homes across the street and next-door. If a person had more than three rooms, sometimes they would have to give up a room to a German military man to occupy it. Those people who had German military men in their home had to be extremely careful about what they did and what they said.

Everything was a bit chaotic. School was closed. Eleni would go to the office to work for her father. Kyria Nitsa did the main cooking and I assisted her. I had the responsibility of cleaning the dishes, the kitchen stove, floors, and bathrooms. Because you could not use money to buy food, Mr. Kounelakis came with me to get what groceries we could find by bartering with a piece of jewelry or some other possession of value. I would assist him in carrying the groceries home. Manoli would go in and out with his friends, or when he did not seem to have much to do he would bother me. On Sundays I was able to get away and spend the day with my Theia Kaliope and my cousins.

When I was able to get there early enough we would go to church together.

The Christmas holidays were bleak. We simply went to church for Divine Liturgy and then came home. There was no caroling and no Christmas cookies, just a quiet exchange of *Merry Christmas*. The months dragged on between the drudgery of the day, the random air raids, hours spent in the bomb shelter, and the continual conversations about the war and what would happen. I myself would keep up with my schooling at night by re-reading my schoolbooks I had from previous years. One of the books I possessed was a German-Greek translator. Between my book and hearing the language spoken all around me, I learned to speak German quite well. I had also taken French for a couple of years in school.

TWO TRAGEDIES

By the fall of 1942 the schools had opened and I was able to return to school. German peacekeeping officers were sent to replace the Gestapo, although a few were remained in strategic areas of the island. I was happy to be in school, and the new German officers seemed to be a bit more civil. When they would come to the door, I could speak to them in German and translate for Kyria Nitsa what they wanted. Usually it was coffee or eggs. Even though she had lost her hearing, Kyria Nitsa was not completely deaf. She was an educated woman and spoke French fluently. Sometimes the German soldiers would come over just looking for someone to talk to, as they must have missed their families back home. I would be the one to translate the conversation between Kyria Nitsa and the German soldiers. At first they mistook me for her daughter because of my level of education and they were surprised to learn that I was the maid.

Earlier that same year, I had learned about a tragedy, either through the newspaper or someone telling me, I can't remember. The tragedy itself I can never forget. It concerns my aunt and uncle. This is my mother's sister, Kaliope, and her husband, John. Prior to the German occupation, my theia and theio lived peacefully in the village of Elia. They had six lovely children and they were a happy family. This was before the fall of 1942 when the Germans were in full control of Crete.

My Theia Kaliope was a nurse who worked in the county hospital in Iraklion. During the war, wounded English, Australian, and New Zealander soldiers arrived at the hospital. My aunt became attached to them while she treated their wounds. She wanted to help them and worked with them to devise a plan to help the soldiers escape, so that that they would not be held as prisoners of war.

As soon as the soldiers were able to stand, she would disguise them by dressing them up in women's clothing. She would then walk them from the hospital to my Uncle John, who would wait outside the gate with a horse and buggy. My theio would then take the soldiers to his home. He would let them stay in his house for a few days, until he could make arrangements to take them to the mountains. In the mountains, the guerrillas would inform the British Royal Navy and make arrangements for their escape back to friendly lines. My theio and theia helped many military men escape this way.

Everything was running well until one night, while my aunt was walking a few men out of the hospital, Nazi soldiers confronted her outside the gate. Some of their own Greek countrymen had betrayed them and given them away. The Nazi's arrested her and the British soldiers. My uncle had just arrived around the corner. He did not have a chance to escape. Two of the Gestapo saw him and caught him at gunpoint. They sent him to a prison in Hania where they later executed him. My aunt was sent to a concentration camp in Auschwitz, Germany, where she suffered indescribable torments and tortures and then was finally executed.

My heart was in agony to learn about the arrest of my theio and theia. When I went home to tell Mr. and Mrs. Kounelakis, they were already aware of the story, but they had no idea that they were related to me. They expressed their sorrow and sympathy for the innocent lives that were being lost.

My cousins were left alone to endure many hardships. As children, they lived in many strange homes and went from one orphanage to another. Years later, after the war, one of her sons established a museum in honor of his parents and others who helped the Allied military forces. The museum is still there to this day.

In the spring of 1943, I received a letter from my Theia Athena from Avdou. She wrote to tell me that my brother Michael was very ill and in the county hospital in Iraklion. She said that I should go to see him immediately. That evening I asked Mr. Kounelakis, "May I have the afternoon off tomorrow to go and see my brother who is ill in the hospital? I have not seen my brother in almost two years since I left him in Arkalohori." Mr. Kounelakis answered, "Yes, you may have the afternoon off."

The next day, after lunch, I got ready and went to the hospital as quickly as I could. As I walked into the hospital, I saw a nurse and asked her if she knew what room my brother was in. She accompanied me to his bed, where he was in a large room with three other patients. As I walked in, I saw my brother was deeply shocked. He looked like the picture of a starving child. My breath was taken away. He had always been a thin boy, but now he looked like a skeleton and his face was yellow. I burst into tears. Nothing could have prepared me for the shock of seeing him so transformed. It was the most dreadful thing imaginable. Although he was still alive, I instantly knew he was dying.

In pain, he took my hand and said, "I love you sister. I have always loved you. Please pray for me that God may take me soon and not let me suffer any longer."

"I cannot believe what you say, Brother. You are so young, only fifteen, and I don't want to lose you. You are my beloved brother and I will pray to God to make you well." I learned that he was diagnosed with leukemia, a disease for which, in those days, there was very little the doctors could do.

After a while I said to him, "I have to go home now but I will be back tomorrow. I will try to bring you some food." I gently kissed him goodbye on his forehead. Traumatized and heartbroken, I cried all the way home. When I left, I went to Anna and Aleko's home. Their mother, Toula, was home from work at the orphanage. I cried as I told them what had happened. Eventually, I found my way to Theia Kaliope and my cousins to let them know. Toula tried to go and see my brother and Theia Kalonika tried to go every other day.

The next day, I brought my brother some chicken soup. He looked toward me and said, "I feel much better seeing you." He took a couple of spoonful of the soup. It was difficult for him to eat. He said, "Thank you, Aristea, it tastes good." When I left, I promised him that I would come back again as often as they would allow me and I told him that Theia Kaliope and Kyria Toula would be coming to visit him also. I kissed him goodbye and told him I would see him soon.

It was difficult for me to keep working without thinking of my brother. Unfortunately, after a short while, Mr. Kounelakis allowed me to go and visit my brother only on Sundays. About a month later, Mr. and Mrs. Kounelakis were invited to a name day celebration. I was asked to accommodate them by assisting the other maid at the home that the name day gathering was at. While I was helping to serve the guests there, I met a lady named Koula. She quietly told me that she had a brother with a small child who needed some assistance if I would like to go and see him. She told me where her brother lived and that the best time to go and see him would be Saturday evenings. I simply said told her that I would possibly go. She gave her brother notice to keep a lookout for me.

The following Saturday I went and met Kyrios Evangelos. I knocked at the door of his home. He opened the door and his little girl was standing with him. I said,

"Hi, I'm Aristea and your sister, Koula, told me to come and see you about helping with your little girl." He invited me in and brought me into the living room where his wife was already seated. He introduced me to his wife. "This is my wife, Zaphyria," he said. His little girl was so sweet and his wife was very beautiful.

Mr. Evangelos asked me what kind of experience I had. I said that I was going to school at the present time. I lost my mother when I was ten years old and I was responsible for taking care of my two brothers and my sister who was a baby. "Well", he said, "you look like you are qualified to take care of my little girl." I explained to him that I could only work after school. "That is fine!" he said in agreement and added, "During the day I have a lady who does the cooking and who cleans the house. Let me show you the house and where your room will be." The house was beautiful and had a very nice balcony from which you could see the Cathedral of Saint Minas. He said, "If you think you would like to come, you can do so on a trial basis." I said, "Thank you very much. I will think about it and let you know soon." I bid his wife and little girl goodbye.

As I walked back to the Kounelakis' I thought that I would like to take this new job, as I would be closer to my brother who was in the hospital. The other motivation for me to take the job was that the Kounelakis' son Manoli was always prodding me by making snide remarks. Manoli was a smart aleck. Many times, he and I would get into arguments about the way he treated me.

The following Friday afternoon was one of those nasty times for Manoli and I. He touted saying, "When I grow up, I will become the captain of a ship and I will hire you to scrub the deck and polish the brass!"

"How do you know that I will not be wealthy enough to leave your parents service when I grow up?" I replied,

"Once you are a servant there is no hope for ever being anything else."

That day, he got under my skin. I told him, "As God is my witness, he will someday justify the wrong and hurt you have caused me." I had strong spirit that would not let me be pushed around, and I had reached my limit. I could scarcely bear the thought of being controlled and humiliated by this young brat. I would tell him that he would be sorry some day and regret the way he treated me. Little did he know that, one day, his father would sign the papers that would give me passage to come to America. But that is another story.

I told Mr. and Mrs. Kounelakis that evening, "I have decided to take another job where I will be closer to my brother who is dying in the hospital. Therefore, I will be leaving tomorrow morning after breakfast." The next morning I packed my suitcase and left. I had faith in God and self-confidence that no matter what happened, I would survive the hardships and something good would come from these difficult times.

On the way to Kyrios Evangelos' home, I wanted to make two stops. One was to see Theia Kaliope to tell her about my new job, and the other was to see my brother. I stopped at Theia Kaliope's first. Theia said to me, "Where are you going with you're suitcase?"

"I have decided to take another job. There is a family who needs help watching their little girl. I liked the little girl immediately. She is well behaved and mature for her age. Theia, I am so glad I found this job. I think it will work out fine. Besides, I will be closer to the hospital, and I can go see my brother more often."

"Well it sounds like it will be better for you. I hope it goes well."

"I better be going because I want to go see Michael at the hospital before I go to Kyrios Evangelos' home." Thea Kaliope gave me some soup to take to Michael and told me to tell him that she would come to visit him after church on Sunday. I thanked her and said goodbye.

I tried to brace myself before entering the room to see my brother. His eyes were closed until I gently touched his arm. "Hi Michael. I am here. I have some good news to tell you. I have taken a new job and I will now be closer to you."

"Hi, Aristea. It is good to see you," he said weakly.

"Theia Kaliope has sent some soup. Do you think you can try to have some now?"

"For you I will try," he answered. I gave him as much as he could take. It was very difficult for him to eat.

After a while I said, "I have to go now to my new job, but tomorrow is Sunday and I will be back. Do you want me to bring you some fruit?"

"If you could bring me some watermelon I think I would like that."

"I will bring you some. Theia Kaliope said that she would come tomorrow as well. I love you brother and I will see you tomorrow."

It took me about twenty minutes to get to Kyrios Evangelos'. It was early afternoon when I arrived. I knocked on the door. A moment later he opened the door.

"Aristea, I thought you were going to send word that you wanted the job? Please, come in."

"I did not have the opportunity to send word, as I have been working hard and I went to visit my brother who is in the hospital in my free time. But, I am here to take the job on a trial basis if you will still have me."

"Of course, please come in. We were just finishing lunch," he said. Little Lena appeared in the living room. She came her father's side and I said, "Hi, Lena. I brought you something." I gave her a doll that my aunt had given to me when I was a little girl. It was in perfect shape. She liked it right away. With that we became friends.

Kyrios Evangelos asked, "Are you hungry? Would you like something to eat?"

"Yes, please. I did not have lunch yet. Thank You," I replied. I set my suitcase down and followed him and Lena into the kitchen where his wife was sitting at the table. His wife said hello, but I noticed that she was very quiet. I was surprised to discover later that Lena's mother was in a state of depression. When I was at the house, the mother would go into the bedroom and close the door. She would stay there for hours. Sometimes I would knock on the door and ask her if she would like to join in a game with her little girl. She looked completely spaced out, as though she was in another world. Finally, she would say, *not now,* and would lock herself in the bedroom again.

Mr. Evangelos was a businessman who specialized in wholesale merchandise. I liked him from the beginning. When he found out that my brother was ill in the hospital, he told me to let him know if there is anything he could do. I told him that I just wanted to be able to go and see him as often as I could. He said that I could go on Sundays and in the evening when he was home. I thanked him for his generosity.

Lena was a very cute little girl with blonde hair and blue eyes. She liked to dance around and play hide and seek. As time went on, I discovered that she liked it when I read little stories to her. Her father was very glad to supply me with lots of children's books.

After lunch, Kyrie Evangelos showed me to my room. This room was small with a window looking at the street, from which I could see the church. An icon of Saint George with the dragon was only one thing that decorated the white wall. This was my first room that had a closet. I was so happy to have my own room again! I thought to myself that this would work out fine. I felt good about my decision to take this new job. I settled down to take an afternoon nap. Hearing Lena at my door awakened me. I guess she came to see what I was doing. I opened the door to find her standing there with the new doll I had given her. I said, "Hi, Lena. Would you like to come in?" She smiled and entered my room. She went over to my suitcase I had left by the door and said, "What is that?" I said, "That is my suitcase with my clothes in it." I put it on the bed and opened it to show her.

The next morning I woke early and thought about going to church. After services I found a small market that was open that had some watermelon. I asked if they could cut it open and make some slices for me so that I could take it to the hospital for my brother. When I got to the hospital my brother's eyes were closed but he was awake and opened them as soon as I got close to his bed. "Hi, Michael I brought you some nice fresh watermelon," I tried to say with a smile, though my heart was aching. "Thank you," he said, "You remembered."

"Of course I remembered. I can never forget you, my brother," I replied. I helped him to sit up a little. He took one bite of the watermelon, but had a difficult time swallowing. I tried to feed him, giving him just a little at a time, and he finished a small slice. Just then Theia Kaliope came in with Marika and Kyriakos.

My Theia turned to Michael, "So I see you are having some watermelon. Is it good?" Michael feebly replied, "Yes Theia. It is sweet, like you." Michael turned to me, "I need to lay down, as I am tired."

"Yes, let me help you. You must get your rest." Theia said, "Well then we will leave so you can sleep. Aristea we will be home if you wish to come and see us later."

"Thank you. I am going to sit here with Michael for now." My family left and I sat down in the chair next to Michael's bed. I turned to Michael and took his hand, saying "I am going to sit here with you until I know that you are comfortable."

"Thank you," he said with tears in his eyes. I got up to kiss him on the forehead once again and told him I loved him. Once I saw that he was sleeping I returned to my new home.

My days were busy, yet pleasant. Despite having school all day and my new job in the afternoons, I felt alone often. I was sorry for Lena, who had a mother who was unable to care for her. There were times when Mr. Evangelos had difficulty calming his wife down, as she would scream and try to jump out of the second floor window. When that occurred I would ask him if I could take Lena with me to stay over at my aunt's house.

I continued my visits to Michael as often as I could, and though I tried to get him to eat and encouraged him that he would get well, he knew otherwise. With every visit I noticed that his eyes grew larger and sunk deeper and deeper into his face. His features grew sharper. When he saw me and knew that I was beside him, he tried to hang on to life as long as he could. On one of the days that I brought him some chicken soup, he could not even eat one spoonful. He weighed less than seventy-five pounds and looked so pale. It was very painful for me to watch my brother fading away, knowing that there was nothing I could do to help. I could not bear another loss, and I could not fight back the tears that rolled down my cheeks every time I had to leave him.

Then one afternoon I came to visit my brother at the hospital with my Theia. We walked into the room, but his bed was empty. The nurse told us he died at one in the afternoon. His body was taken to the basement where he would be placed in a roughly made wooden coffin. The nurse told us that the hearse would be coming to get his body. My theia and I quickly went out of the hospital and waited by the front doors for the black horse-drawn hearse to come.

At just seventeen, my life had been uprooted and torn apart so many times. I remember praying at the burial of my twin siblings. I was uprooted from my house in the middle of the night and had lost my mother when I was just ten years old. The Germans executed my aunt and uncle, I had already lived through three years of terror with the German occupation, and now my brother was dead as well.

The hearse suddenly appeared, interrupting my thoughts. The coachman went directly inside the hospital, not knowing who we were. About ten minutes later, which seemed like an eternity, they emerged from the hospital with the rough wooden coffin. My Theia and I started sobbing and crying out, "May God give him rest! May God forgive him!" I cried out to my brother, "May God rest your soul and may we see each other in heaven someday." Tears poured down my cheeks as the pain was choking me. At that moment I wish I could have died with him. Once they closed the door to the hearse, the coachman got in his seat and started away. I tried to follow him but he was too fast. Theia came to me and put her arms around me and said, "We will never be able to walk fast enough to follow him." I collapsed into her chest sobbing. I would never know where my brother was buried. That was the last I saw of my brother Michael. The memories of the life we lived together as children will stay with me forever.

1943: A NIGHT OF TERROR

One day just before school let out for the summer, Mr. Evangelos made me an offer. "Aristea," he said, "my little girl loves you so much that I think she would be very unhappy without you. I would appreciate it very much if you would consider going to my sister's home in the village to take care of Lena for the summer. I have already decided it would be better for her at my sister's house and I know if you were there to take care of her, she would not be so lonely. I will pay you double for this. I have a lot of confidence in you and for this reason I will not worry about my little girl. I will remain here in the city to take care of my wife. She is in a treatment program that I have to pursue, hoping to God that she will get better." I could tell that Mr. Evangelos loved his wife very much and he was extremely worried about her condition.

I agreed to go and take care of Lena for the summer. However, I made it clear that I must return to Iraklion by the end of August to register for school and Mr. Evangelos agreed. I spoke to my Theia Kaliope that evening about

Mr. Evangelos' offer. She said, "It is a good idea to go with Lena to her aunt's village. It will benefit the child to have you there." So, at the end of the school year, Lena and I went to live with Mr. Evangelos' sister, Koula, who lived in the village of Skaloni. Mr. Evangelos and his wife remained in Iraklion. He would be taking his wife to a doctor for psychiatric evaluations.

That summer was exceedingly hot. During the month of July the temperatures remained over a hundred degrees and the night temperatures did not drop much. Most people slept in their courtyards. One hot night, around midnight, when I was sleeping on an old wooden sofa in the courtyard, I heard the noise of military boots approaching. At first I thought that I was having a nightmare. Then a German soldier shined a flashlight in my face and pointed a gun at me. "*Steigen gehen!*" (Arise to go), he shouted. I spoke some German, so I asked him, where to go. I was trembling all over and shaking so much that I could hardly stand. He shouted at me to go to the plaza.

I didn't know what they wanted of me. I noticed that Koula was behind me carrying Lena. When I got to the plaza there were already men, women, and children there. Many of them were still only half dressed. The children and women were crying and terrified. I thought that we would all be killed- that this night would be the end of my life. One of the German Gestapo soldiers that guarded us looked compassionate, so I worked up the courage to ask him, "Why did they bring all of us to the plaza?"

He said, "You will soon find out." Our terror grew

with each second. Within a short time, they separated the men in one line and the women and children into another. Then they took the men and marched them at gunpoint to the main road, where empty military trucks were waiting. As we watched the men being loaded into the trucks, we began to weep, not knowing what would happen to them. The Germans left with our men and we were left standing there in shock until we heard a voice saying, "Go to the church, go to the church." It was the voice of the village priest. He had been sleeping among the grape vines, and the German Gestapo did not see him. We all went to the church and prayed with tears in our eyes that the Lord would keep the men safe.

Early the next morning, some mothers sent a group of teenage boys to ask the people in the surrounding area if they saw a group of Greek men in German trucks. Some of them said they had seen some civilians working to break rocks to off a road ten miles to the south. The boys walked the five miles and sure enough, they saw their fathers working on the road breaking rocks. The men were so happy to see the boys. Their fathers said that they had worked all day in the blistering heat with very little to eat or drink. Some of them collapsed from sunstroke, while others had suffered from blisters on their hands from breaking the rocks all day.

The boys returned home and told their mothers what they discovered. The women understood the situation and immediately got together to prepare food and water, and then walked the five miles to bring it to their men. This continued for a few days. One night, while the guards were talking to each other, some of the men seized the opportunity to escape into the hills. Fortunately, we did not suffer any repercussions from the Gestapo as a result of their escape.

FACING THE GESTAPO

Life in Skalani continued to be tense. The women had organized themselves into groups to rotate who would make the long walk to provide sustenance for the men. The Gestapo, who occupied the elementary school, would come into the village unannounced, seeking olive oil, eggs, and chickens. Water sources were shut off except for a three-hour period every day, which would always begin at a random time.

Some weeks later, the Gestapo left the elementary school and was replaced with German peacekeeping soldiers. Our water continued to be controlled and they continued to come to the village at random times to obtain food supplies. They were a bit more civil in that they were willing to exchange bread for the things they wanted from us. We did not have bread, so it was a welcome exchange. Thus, we tried to go on with our daily live as best we could.

One day around noon, I was in the plaza waiting in line to get water, when a black limousine pulled up. I knew it was the German police by the swastika on the side of the car. They parked the limousine under a shady tree and two

German policemen came out from the car followed by a civilian man who was an interpreter.

They approached the women who were in line filling their jugs with water and asked, "Do you know a young girl by the name, Aristea Vasiloyianakis?" I was right there and I couldn't hide. Terrified, I said, "That is my name." The Gestapo officer immediately grabbed me by the arm and dragged me to the car. He shoved me in the back seat and closed the door.

I realized that they were taking me to the Gestapo headquarters, but I couldn't imagine why. My mind was racing. What did they want from me? What did I do to deserve this? I could not believe that this was happening to me. I was sitting there in the back seat of their police car completely horrified. The police officer finally said through the interpreter that they were taking me to their headquarters in Iraklion for questioning, but he did not say why.

As we drove to Iraklion I was shaking and my heart was beating so hard I thought I was going to have a heart attack. Finally, we arrived at the Gestapo headquarters, which was in the city hall. They opened the car door and let me out and yelled at me, "Get going." One Gestapo officer was in front of me and another was behind me with the interpreter. They brought me into an office where an SS Officer was standing behind his desk, waiting for our arrival. He appeared to be a colonel. The colonel was a big man with reddish hair and blue eyes. He wore a metallic chain with a medallion hanging from it around his neck.

The medallion had an embossed eagle along with a swastika. Standing in the room with him was another officer who was his assistant. I did not know his rank. I observed that they both had the swastika on the sleeves of their uniforms. The colonel dismissed the two policemen who brought me in, so that I was alone with the colonel, his assistant, and the interpreter. There was a single empty chair in the middle of the room. The assistant shoved me into the chair. I still had no idea why I was there. I was trembling all over and am I still amazed that I did not collapse from fear. My guardian angel was with me.

The colonel held a black baton in his hand addressed me with his first question, hitting the desk with his baton. He looked directly at my face but paused for the interpreter to translate the question. Fortunately, because I knew German I could understand everything he was saying. I intentionally held my head down and did not look at him so that he could not pick up any trace that I understood what he was saying. In this way, while the interpreter was translating in Greek, I had a moment to prepare my response. He asked, "What is your full name?" His assistant was seated at this point taking notes.

I answered in Greek, "Aristea Vasilogianakis." He continued to question me while firmly banging the shiny black baton against his desk. A quick image popped into my mind of Mr. Kounelakis, the attorney, who spoke about his legal work. I remembered him saying that if you are defending yourself, your story must always remain the same, it must be consistent. I tried very hard to stay firm.

"I understand you work for Mr. Evangelos and take care of his little girl. How long have you been with the family?" he asked.

"Just a few months."

"What kind of man is Mr. Evangelos?"

"He is very kind and generous, especially to needy people."

"What kind of business does he operate?"

I began to understand that they chose to question me because of my relationship with Mr. Evangelos. However, I had yet to understand what his crime was. What was the catalyst for this interrogation? I told him what I knew. "He usually works in an office tending to his import-export enterprise of raisins, soap, oil, and various other products." After two hours of repeated questioning, the door behind me banged open and two Gestapo brought Mr. Evangelos into the room. They gave him a chair to sit down near the colonel. Mr. Evangelos looked very weak and disturbed. I don't think they gave him much to eat. He looked like he had lost weight and his face was pale. I was shocked to see him in this condition, which made me even more afraid. I was terrified of what they would do to me or where they might take me.

The colonel began to question Mr. Evangelos with greater intensity, yelling at him. They probed him with questions about his life. I am sure that he had already answered these questions, but they were hoping he would slip up. What were they after?

The colonel yelled, "We searched your house and

found a radio in your attic! We have a witness that knows you to have said that you listen to the radio often. You get information from military sources from Cairo and you secretly report the messages to the guerrillas in the mountains!" He continued yelling and waving the baton in Mr. Evangelos' face. "We know that you are a spy and we have sources that have informed us!"

Mr. Evangelos tried to defend himself saying, "I rented this flat three years ago. I never saw a radio or knew there was a radio in the attic. I never had a reason to go up there for anything. I am a very busy man with a business and an ill wife." He calmly said, "I am afraid that the person who gave you this information is big liar."

The colonel snapped, "Perhaps Aristea Vasiloyianakis, who has been working for you the past few months heard the radio playing." The colonel turned to me and repeated the question about the radio. I answered, "I never heard or saw or knew of any radio." They interrogated us all day without food and water. I felt the colonel getting angry with me, repeating the same questions over and over.

The colonel tried to fabricate a story to get Mr. Evangelos to confess. "Aristea heard you listening to the radio in the attic after dinner!" he said. I hastened to answer by saying, "Mr. Evangelos was always with us after dinner. He never went into the attic." Like a lightened bolt out of nowhere the colonel slapped me hard on both cheeks, yelling, "Shut up! You will only answer questions when you are asked."

After hours of being interrogated and being beaten, my

face was swelling and my left eye became completely closed. Exasperated with us, the colonel screamed for the policemen outside to come in and take me away. The two SS policemen walked me outside and started to walk me down the street. When I asked them where they were taking me, they firmly told me not to ask. After walking about a half mile, we stood in front of the city jail. Inside there was a Greek policeman who checked me in. He asked me for my name and had me sign a paper acknowledging that I had been admitted to the jail. He asked me if I had any family living in the city. I asked him if they could send someone to notify my aunt and told him where she lived. A Greek policeman came to escort me to the jail, while the two SS policemen followed to make sure the Greek policeman locked me in. The SS men left saying, "We'll see you tomorrow for further questioning."

I found myself in an empty jail cell that was about six by eight feet and seven feet high. There was no toilet and no water. The floor was cement and had a small hole in the middle with a metal plate over it, which was the toilet. The chain of about twelve jail cells made a U shape and in the middle was a dirt courtyard. There was a mulberry tree in the center of the courtyard and four benches underneath it formed an unconnected square. The bars of the cell were open in the front and a small open-air window was in the back. Solid walls divided each cell. You had to bang the cell door for someone to come and take you to the bathroom. If you couldn't wait, you had to use the hole in the middle of your cell floor.

I sat on the floor with my hands trembling. I felt feverish and weak and I could not open my left eye. My cheeks were burning from the swelling. I was in a nightmare. All I could do was look up to heaven and I cry with my heart, "Father, you know the horror I am going through. Please deliver me from this horrible situation."

After a short while, the Greek police officer, Kyrios Georgos, brought me a cold rag for my face and a straw mattress. He said, "I don't know why they brought you here. They look for excuses to arrest anyone. I know that you are innocent." I was so exhausted and worn out that I slept for fourteen hours. I woke up around ten the next morning and someone brought me water and a piece of dry bread. Around noon my heart received a boost of encouragement when I saw my aunt in the courtyard. She was devastated to find me all beaten up. She exclaimed, "Oh, my Lord, I have seen many things, but I never expected to find you here in this situation. What happened?" I explained the whole story. She asked, "How long will you be in here?"

"Theia I have no idea. We will have to wait and see," I replied. "Please say a prayer for me as I am so fearful that they could send me to a concentration camp in Poland."

"Please don't say that. I could never swallow the idea of that happening to you. I will go to Saint Titus church tonight to light a candle and pray for you. Do you know what jail they took Mr. Evangelos to, so that I may go and see him too?"

"No, I don't know where they took him."

They brought me back two or three more times that week to interrogate me alone, without Mr. Evangelos. The last time that they brought me in for questioning, the colonel actually apologized to me saying, "I'm sorry I had to hit you, but you must remain in jail until I complete a full investigation."

The days following the interrogations were a living hell. I didn't know what would happen to me. It took about ten days before the swelling in my eye went down and I could open it. After about a week I remembered a policeman who was a friend of my father's. Eventually, they allowed my jail cell door to be left open so that I could walk around the courtyard at leisure. When the Greek policeman brought in a visitor one day, I approached him and said, "Excuse me, Kyrios Georgos, may I talk to you for a moment?"

"Yes, Aristea what is it?" he asked. We walked over and sat down on one of the benches under the mulberry tree. I said to him, "I remembered a friend of my fathers who is a policeman. Do you think that you can contact him to see if he can help me?"

"What is his name?" he asked.

"Kyrios Filipakis." I said.

Kyrios Georgos looked surprised, "I know him and he is a very good friend of mine. Don't worry I will get in touch with him"

"Thank you very much, I appreciate your help and I know that God will bless you for what you are doing for me today." With this new hope, my spirit soared and before I lay my head down that night, I prayed, "Thank you for guiding me. Please, Lord, guide these people with the wisdom to help bring about my freedom."

The visitations of my friends kept my courage up. My cousins Marika and Kyriakos visited me, cried with me, and bore my pain. They would bring me baked vegetables, rice pilaf, or french fries with salad. My friends Aleko and Anna also came with their mother Toula, who brought me grapes and watermelon. All of them said that they were praying for my release and hoped that the policeman that my father knew would help. Koula had come from the village and brought some of my clothes to me. She told me that Kyria Zaphyria's parents were staying with her and that she was keeping Lena with her at her home. Theia Kaliope generously offered to take my clothes and wash them and bring them back for me. I was so thankful that they were able to visit me during this insufferable time.

After six weeks of living hell, my day of liberation arrived when the chief of police himself came to give me the good news that I was free. Kyrios Georgos said, "It is a miracle that you are out. I hope that everything will work out for you in your future and I wish you good luck. Please come to see me if you need any further help." The chief of police explained to me that he went himself to speak to the colonel. He said that he knew me and that I had worked for an attorney and was a good citizen." He said that the SS colonel responded by saying, "Yes, our investigation does not show any evidence that she was involved with any espionage. She can be released." The Chief of Police asked the colonel for a letter clearing and releasing me from jail. The colonel had his assistant write the letter with an official seal. With tears in my eyes, I hugged him and thanked him for all his hard work to negotiate my freedom. I said, "I will never forget what you did for me and I hope same day I can repay you. Deep down in my heart I knew it was a miracle that I was free at last.

As soon as I was released I practically ran to Theia Kaliope's house. When I knocked on the door my Theia answered. As soon as she saw me she grabbed me and held me crying, "Glory to God, glory to God you are here! I can't believe I am seeing you." Marika and Kyriakos were right behind her. They brought me inside and we all huddled together, hugging each other with grateful hearts. I remained with them for a few weeks to recuperate and think about my future.

Koula found out that I was released from jail and she came with Lena to find me at my theia's house. When Lena saw me she crawled into my lap where I was sitting and gave me a hug and said in her little voice, "I want you to come home with me." Koula asked me if I would consider coming to live at her house and continue watching Lena, as the little girl missed me. She expressed how grateful she would be herself if I would come. I told her that I would come within two weeks. I later found out from Koula that the SS accused her brother, Kyrios Evangelos of espionage and sentenced him to go to a prison in Hania.

THE ABDUCTION OF A GENERAL

I first heard this story about the abduction of a German general when I visited the village of my cousin, George, not far from Iraklion, in the fall of 1944. George delighted in telling this story, which he himself witnessed while tending his grapevines on a Cretan hillside. "I have to tell you the story" he began, " I was there and I saw it with my own eyes!" He continued, " What took place, no one could have imagined that this could have occurred without someone getting shot. It was astonishing!" Not only was George a witness to this event, but also he was a close friend of the local people employed at the villa where the German general resided.

The story begins in the spring of 1944. The British officers who were working with the Greek military and Cretan Guerillas received word from Cairo stating that British SOE Major Patrick Leigh Fermor was going to drop by parachute into the Cretan mountains alone, despite great personal risk. The mission was to kidnap the German General-lieutenant Friedrich-Wilhelm Muller who was stationed in Crete. General Muller committed many atrocities during his command on the island of Crete. During the organization of the plans to kidnap General Muller, General major Heinrich Kreipe replaced him.

Major Fermor and his assistant Captain William Moss together with the Cretan guerrillas proceeded with their plans regardless of the change in German command. Major Fermor together with Captain Moss and their Cretan cohorts left the safety of the mountains in the middle of the night. They went to the village to determine the exact location of General Kreipe's headquarters. For several days, they studied the route he took from his headquarters to the villa where he lived.

The villa, only a few miles from the general's headquarters, was near Knossos Palace, the backyard of my childhood home. After much study, Fermor asked his guerilla friends if they could obtain two German uniforms, one for him and one for his assistant Captain Moss. They would disguise themselves as German military policemen.

The other team players in the abduction consisted of eleven men, five of whom were Cretan. One of the Cretan men was a valuable team player for several reasons. He grew up in the area and was familiar with Knossos as well at the terrain. He also happened to be a good friend of the general's driver. In fact, he once attended a celebration at the villa where the general now lived. He was also a friend with one of the British officers.

The group carefully worked out the details of their mission. The general's headquarters were in the village of

Archanes, a few miles south of Knossos. The men strategically staged a routine traffic control point on a hairpin turn in the road. When General Kreipe was en route, Fermor and Moss who were dressed as German military policemen stopped him at this position.

My cousin retells his story saying it was just before dusk. The men were divided into two groups and hid among the bushes on both sides waiting for the General to arrive. The British officers dressed as German policemen and stopped the car. One of the disguised British officers approached the General to ask for his identification, while the other knocked out the driver and pulled him out of the car. Quickly the guerillas removed the General's jacket, put handcuffs on him and pushed him into the back seat of the car. The British officer then put on the general's coat and moved into the front passenger seat of the vehicle.

They then drove the general to the south side of Crete, abandoned the car in the last village they came to, and took a path leading into the mountains. The British left a letter and some other items that would make it appear that it was strictly a British operation, thus protecting the Cretan people from any retribution for this abduction.

Arriving at their destination by dawn, the British soldiers hid the general in a cave, where Cretan men guarded him. Meanwhile, German airplanes dropped leaflets announcing the destruction of villages if they did not set the general free. The British officers stood firm and did not give up their captive. They held the general hostage reporting to Cairo that they held the general in an undisclosed location and would retain him there until they were ready to retrieve him. On May 14, 1944 he was taken by a British motor-launch and transported to Egypt. Unfortunately, the German military held to their warning, and removed people from four different villages, confiscating all of their goods and burned the villages to the ground. As refugees they came to the city seeking help from their countrymen and the Red Cross. Many of them were seen sleeping on the sidewalks.

This unique, daring and courageous mission crumbled the German morale on Crete as the war had already been turning on the Eastern front for almost a year and the D-Day invasion was only a few weeks away. Years later, a book was written by one of the British operatives, Stanley Moss, called *Met By Moonlight*. It was adapted into a film in 1957.

Nothing makes me smile when I recall this era of my youth, but I can't help but smile whenever I picture my cousin, sitting at the table in the plaza, sipping his Greek coffee, and bragging about the time he witnessed the abduction of a German General.

LIBERATED AT LAST

After the German invasion in 1941, life in Greece almost stood still. In particular, on my beloved island of Crete, many of my fellow Cretans suffered heavily from the Nazi tyranny. In the first month of the occupation alone, the Nazi army executed 2,500 civilians and burned six villages.

Many of us lived in schoolhouses while other slept on the sidewalks. Although physically restrained, the Cretan spirit never rested. We pressed forward with forbearance and focused on our freedom. The spirit of the Greek people has endured through many wars in the past four thousand years, and Hitler's army did not stop us from having determination and hope that we would defeat the Germans in the end. A famous Greek patriot once said, "Greek people stood for the undeniable moral claim that there are certain values in this world that are so precious, and so sacred, that they cannot be compromised at any cost; there values are those of liberty and freedom."

During the duration of the occupation of Crete, the

Greek guerrillas never stopped fighting the Germans. The guerillas kept in close comunication with the Allies by short wave radio. Kyrios Evangelos was one of the people who risked his life to listen to the radio and provide information to the resistance. After the war, I visited Mr. Evangelos in his office. He was skin and bones. He said to me that the Gestapo had scheduled to send him to a prison in Poland. He thanked God the Germans left and that he was freed. I thanked God that his life was spared and that even though I suffered the interrogations, beating, and jail, perhaps through my suffering I contributed to his life being spared.

Beginning in June of 1944, when we heard that the American troops were winning the battle on different fronts, it gave us hope that freedom was coming soon. In September of that year, the German Army finally left Iraklion without so much as shooting one more bullet. The citizens of Iraklion could not believe what they were seeing. When they realized that the Germans were leaving to defend their own country, men, women and children thronged the avenues of Iraklion, joyfully screaming and shouting, "At last we are free!" Joyous celebration and spontaneous parades and marches continued for days. Crete was in a state of jubilant chaos led mainly by the guerrillas.

During this period, war trials were taking place at the courthouse building. Those who had collaborated with the Germans in murdering civilians were sent to life imprisonment. However, the guerrillas in attendance wanted them to be sentenced to death. The guerrillas took these traitors and beheaded them, throwing their heads and bodies outside the window of the courthouse. While I did not witness the bodies being thrown out, I did see the blood dripping down the outside beneath the window. The bloodstained walls remained there for a long time as a reminder to the people that the sentence for traitors was death. This horrific sight shocked me and I gasped when I saw it and realized what was happening. These are part of the memories of war that I wish could be erased from my mind, but these dramas are hard to forget.

The celebration parades continued on. My friends and I watched as people marched through the streets, waving flags. The church bells rang out joyously, cannons boomed, and men with trumpets descended from the hills, playing freedom songs. I was overtaken with the emotion of the people, and burst into tears. A battleground had turned into a celebration. After four years of vigilantly enduring executions, tortures, imprisonments, slave labor, and terrorization, after four years of surviving on dandelion greens, olives, and snails, we were a free nation once again.

A VISIT WITH YIAYIA AND REUNION WITH MY BROTHER

As time went on, things quieted down and the government began to restore order. The buses once again ran on their normal schedules. I thought to myself that the time seemed right for me to go and visit my brother, Eleftherios, who was living in the village with our yiayia. I had not seen him in two years. I was still living with Koula and Lena at the time. I asked Koula if she would mind if I took a leave for a few weeks to go see my brother and Yiayia in Avdou. The years may go by and things may change, but my love for my brother is for eternity. I had not heard news from my brother for what seemed like ages. With the war going on, there were no telephones to use and communication and travel was difficult, if not impossible. You cannot imagine how good it felt to be able to ride the bus again and travel freely without terror around us.

Before I bought a ticket for my trip, I went to a

yardage store to buy material for my yiayia and brother. I purchased enough material to make a dress for Yiayia and a suit with two pairs of pants for my brother.

The following day, I boarded the bus to the village Avdou. I anticipated seeing my brother but wondered what condition I might find him in after the trauma of losing our mother and the horrors of the war. After getting off the bus at the square, I walked the rest of the way to Yiayia's house. As I was approaching the familiar neighborhood, I saw Yiayia in the distance drawing water from the well. I ran to her and gave her a big hug and kiss. My brother saw me and came running. With tears in his eyes he hugged and kissed me. He said, "I thought when the Germans left Iraklion you might come to see me, but I didn't think it would be this soon!"

You cannot imagine how I felt when I saw my brother after being separated for so long. He was so grown up and even his voice had changed. However, I was shocked when I saw how thin he was, so thin that I thought he might be sick as Antonti had been. I soon realized that his gauntness was due to the starvation he endured through the war.

Eleftherios said, "I am so glad to see you. You must be tired and hungry. Let's go inside and get something to eat." He led me inside to where my yiayia was preparing dinner. She had some homemade noodles and I made a sauce to go over them. Yiayia brought out cheese, bread, and freshly cut grapes from the vine, and we talked into the night about what we endured through the past two years since we had last seen each other.

The next morning we enjoyed Yiayia's *loukoumathes*. She poured lots of honey and sprinkled cinnamon and chopped nuts on top. We enjoyed the warmth of the *loukoumathes* as well as the warmth of being together again. After breakfast Eleftherios and I went to see the tailor about having a suit made for him. The tailor took my brother's measurements and said, "Come back in four days to try it on and see if any adjustments need to be made."

I asked the tailor, "Do you think there might be enough material leftover to make a second pair of pants?"

"After I finish with the suit, I will see," he replied.

That afternoon I took Eleftherios to the barbershop because he had contracted lice and had to have his head shaved, as this was the only way to get rid of the lice. I don't think he had a hair cut since the war started. When we returned I asked Yiayia if we could heat some water for Eleftherios to take a bath.

Four days later, Eleftherios and I went back to the tailor for the fitting. The tailor said, "He will look like a new man when I finish sewing it. Come back in ten days and it will be ready." When we returned Eleftherios put on the suit and came out with a big smile, his voice was filled with gratitude, saying, "Thank you Aristea, it fits me perfectly!" When my Yiayia saw him all dressed up in the suit she said, "He looks as if has grown into a man overnight!" When we sat down to have dinner that evening, I made a proposition to my brother. "Eleftherios," I said, " I came to the village for two reasons. One was to visit with you and Grandmother and to have the tailor make you new clothing. The other reason is I would like you to come with me to the city because, as you can see, there are no jobs for you here. You will have better opportunities to get work there or to go to school to learn a trade. I would like for you to think about this seriously"

I stayed a total of two weeks at Grandmother's. I was glad to see her but it was time for me to return to Iraklion. I had an appointment with a dress designer to discuss if I could attend classes in exchange for some housework. It was my greatest desire to go to a trade school and learn how to design and create my own patterns for sewing clothe. In the thirties and forties, readymade clothing did not exist in Iraklion. A dressmaker or a tailor made most of the clothing. If you were a good dressmaker, you could have a successful business and make a living. As I grew older, I was attracted to clothing design, especially the new fashions that came from Paris. I wanted with all my heart to attend a trade school to obtain my certificate in fashion design. This is why it was so important to me that I keep the appointment with the lady at the trade school.

As I was getting ready to leave for Iraklion, my brother approached me and gave me a hug and said, "I have decided to come with you to the city. I realize that what you said to me makes sense." For the first time since the war began, my spirit swelled with hope for the possibilities that lay ahead of my brother and I.

ASPIRATIONS

Eleftherios and I left Avdou together. It was sad for Yiayia to see us leave, but I promised her that we would come back to celebrate Christmas together. We boarded the bus at six in the evening and when we arrived in Iraklion, Aunt Kaliope was waiting for us at the bus stop. We hailed a taxi to take us to Aunt Kaliope's house. I knew that whenever I needed a place to stay, Aunt Kaliope's house was open to me. It was good to be together with our cousins Marika and Kyriakos. My cousins were more like a brother and sister to me than cousins. Marika and I loved each other and bonded like glue. As things began to return to normal, we once again enjoyed going to the plaza with the *Lions Fountain* with our brothers.

I offered to pay my aunt a small fee for room and board while we stayed there but she refused to accept anything. I had some money because I saved most of what I earned while working for Mr. Evangelos the previous two years. I had it in mind to use some of that money for an apartment for my brother and I.

242

I went to see Koula and Lena a few days after I returned to Iraklion. When I arrived Lena was sleeping so I only saw Koula. I was glad that Lena was sleeping, as I did not want to have to say goodbye to her and see her cry. I explained to Koula that my brother had returned to Iraklion with me and that we were going to rent an apartment together, so I would no longer be staying with her to take care of Lena. However, I promised to visit as often as I could.

After looking for a month, I found a small apartment in a nice neighborhood. It had one room with a small kitchen attached and enough area to accommodate a table and chairs. We moved in as soon as I found a wagon to carry our belongings to the apartment. We didn't have much furniture at first, so we slept on the cement floor. Eventually I purchased two beds and a table with four chairs from the local flea market. Aunt Kaliope supplied us with pots and pans and a few dishes.

The courtyard of our apartment had an outdoor fireplace with a chimney made of clay and stone, where we could heat water for laundry and bathing. We also used it for cooking. I purchased a small barbeque to grill food, which we heated using coke wood, as there were no charcoal briquettes. We would cook stews and vegetables in a pot or make french fries in a frying pan. We rarely had meat. The courtyard also had a couple of trees spread far enough apart to stretch a rope to dry laundry on.

We slowly began to meet our neighbors. One lady, Amalia, lived across the street and was very kind to me. She was married to an attorney and had two sons who both became doctors. She and I became very good friends and our friendship played a very important role in my life, especially when I met my husband, Floyd.

Eleftherios and I had to face many disappointments and challenges during the first few months in our new apartment – especially Eleftherios. He hoped to find a job as a busboy in a coffee shop and began to search for work in various places, but by the end of the day, he would come home exhausted and discouraged. He almost gave up. I tried to encourage him by saying, "Don't worry, you're smart and something is bound to come up soon." He said. "It better be soon, because I am exhausted from walking the streets to no avail."

One evening, when he returned home after another failed job search, he said to me, "After dinner, I would like to talk with you about a venture I would like to undertake. I would like your opinion." We finished dinner quickly. I was anxious to hear what venture my brother wished to discuss. He sat me down and began, "While I was out walking today searching for work from store to store, I came across a gentleman who sold newspapers and magazines on a busy street corner in front of a shop. I asked him how his business was doing. He said he was making enough money to support his family and provide food for the table every day. And then an idea came to me. I know that my friend, Aleko, has an old baby buggy in his shed. I am sure that if I ask him he would gladly give it to me. I am thinking about building a square box with separate compartments where I can place miscellaneous items such as crochet needles, spools of thread, gum, candy, cigarettes, and other sundries. I think I can make a successful business. First thing tomorrow morning I'll go and see Aleko about the baby buggy." I was very proud of his ingenuity and willingness to find a way to make money at such a young age.

"This is a wonderful idea," I told him, "In the meantime, I will go to see the instructor at the trade school."

The next morning, I met the instructor at her workshop and she showed me around. She had twelve girls working for her sewing dresses. She introduced me to them saying, "You may have a new student joining the class." After she showed me the shop, she took me into her office to talk business. She asked what my goal was and I expressed my desire to become a certified fashion designer.

I informed her that I would do my best to learn the trade, but at present, I could not afford to pay for even the first semester's tuition. I said, "I am an excellent cook and have a lot of experience in housework. I would like to work for you in exchange for attending a half day of trade school classes." Since she did not have time to cook and clean her house, she thought this was a wonderful idea and wrote up an agreement. I was to start the very next day.

I had been attending classes for about three months when my Uncle Michael came to visit us. When he learned that I wanted to be a dress designer he made a promise to me. He said, "When things stabilize in Europe, I would like to send you to Paris to finish there and get a Parisian certificate in design."

I said, "Thank you, Uncle Michael. I am delighted at your offer. If I go to Paris to attend school and if my business does well, I will repay you double whatever expenses you incur on my behalf." I could finally dream once more and I could see my dreams becoming a reality. I began dressmaking classes and Eleftherios, at the age of fifteen, became a businessman.

My Brother Elefterios with his push cart he used to sell kiosk items.

WHEN I FIRST MET FLOYD

After the Germans left Crete, the U.S. military sent peacekeeping troops to stabilize the island. We were so excited to have the Americans on Crete.

It was on a sunny afternoon near the beginning of October in 1945. My friend, Eleni, came by our apartment and asked if I wanted to accompany her to the park for a walk. Having little else to do, I gladly accepted. That afternoon I was wearing a navy blue skirt and a white silk blouse with tiny little roses on it. My hair was well groomed and adorned with a jasmine garland, which gave off a heavenly aroma.

After we walked at the park for a while, we decided to go to an outdoor restaurant and order some refreshments. We ordered the traditional *gazoza*. We sat down by a table and watched the people go by. While we were sipping our soda and enjoying a little music played by local musicians, a young lady approached Eleni and motioned for her to follow. Eleni said to me, "Wait here, I'll be back in ten minutes." She came back and said, "Come with me, I want you to meet my friend." We left the restaurant and I followed her down the street.

Standing at the side of the road were two of Eleni's girlfriends, Aliki and Zoe. To my surprise they were standing next four American soldiers who were there with their military truck. They were all dressed in their best uniforms, which were decorated with all their medals for their achievements. Aliki and Zoe, who spoke English, introduced us to the American soldiers. One of them was Floyd Pettis, who was the driver of the American military vehicle. The men wanted to know if we could direct them to a nice restaurant to have dinner, and then they invited us to join them. We said there was an outdoor restaurant a little distance from the Minoan Palace. They said that would be great and we accepted the invitation.

The restaurant was set among grape vines. The waiter sat us at a table near a window with a view of a rose garden. The men ordered ouzo, appetizers, and a chicken dinner. Everyone was enjoying the ouzo and the music playing on the Victrola while waiting for the chicken dinner. We had arrived around seven in the evening and I noticed that it was almost nine and the dinner had still not been served. I began to worry about getting home before my brother found out that I was missing, which may result in him questioning me as to where I had been so late at night.

Finally, I went into the kitchen to inquire about the long delay. I asked the cook why it was taking so long to prepare the dinner. The answer came back, "Lady, we had to catch the chicken, butcher her, pluck the feathers, and then cook the chicken. All of that takes time to prepare!"

However, I could not wait any longer so I asked Aliki to ask Floyd if he would take me home. Since Floyd was the driver, he gladly agreed to take me home. When we approached the outskirts of the town, I mentioned to him where to stop. So he stopped by the cemetery and I walked rest of the way home. Eleni came with me, but she went back with Floyd. When I got home I thanked God that my brother was not there. I was safe for now.

Some days later, Eleni and I were out again in the evening, promenading in front of the public gardens. To our surprise, we saw Floyd and his friend Brady coming along the road in their military vehicle. They stopped to unload some Greek men who worked on the US base. They were Greek men who had lived in America before the war began. They had come to Greece to visit their families. While they were visiting, the war broke out and they could not return to America. The American military hired them to work on the base, as they spoke English very well.

As soon as Floyd saw us he said "Hello girls, good to see you." Floyd introduced us to one of the Greek men named, John. He asked John to translate a request to us. John then said in Greek, "He would like to take a walk with you girls together with his friend, Brady." I replied, "Provided that Eleni comes with me. We will meet them at the outskirts of the town near the cemetery." I did not want to take the chance of one of my brother's friends seeing us with American soldiers and gossip beginning. They agreed and we began to walk on the right side of the street and Floyd and his friend walked on the left side of the street. A short time later, we met at the designated area. Floyd took me by the hand and we walked up and down the path, but we did not say anything, as neither of us understood the others' language.

It was a wonderful night with a clear sky with a bright full moon. His hands felt so warm to mine; as my hands were always cold he tried to warm them. He was trying to say something to me and he took some candy bars from his pocket and put them in mine. He looked at his watch and showed me *seven*, trying to say that he would like to see me the next evening at seven. I spoke German well, and I understood the word *seben* in English would be seven. So I said, "Yes, I will meet you at seven."

When Eleni and I returned home to my apartment, we sat down to enjoy the two candy bars Floyd placed in my pocket. We unwrapped them and placed the wrappers in the ashtray on the table. We thoroughly enjoyed our American treat, as we discussed what a thrilling evening it had been with Floyd and Brady.

MY BROTHER AND THE FIREWOOD

The next morning, when I woke up I asked my brother, "Eleftherios, can you go and buy some wood to heat the water so we can wash some clothes today?" He said, "The American soldier who gave you the chocolate candy bars is the one you should ask to buy the wood!"

I said, " I was not with an American soldier. Those wrappers came from a friend of Eleni's who gave the candy to her."

"You can't tell me that," he replied angrily. "Those kind of candy bars are not sold in the stores!" While we were arguing back and forth, Eleftherios took a piece of wood and hit my leg to the point that the pain shocked me. My friend, Eleni, found me bleeding and me hobbled. She went to look for help and found Floyd, whom she told what happened.

Determined to find me, Floyd left his military truck parked, and began to secretly follow Eleni from a distance. Eleni returned to my house and was telling me how she saw Floyd and explained to him the situation. Then we heard a knock at the door. Eleni got up to open the door, at which point she almost fainted when she saw Floyd standing there. He rushed in uninvited and came to me and found my leg swollen with a two-inch gouge. It was immediately clear that he was stunned to find me in such a condition. Using his watch, he pointed to nine and said *doctor*. I quickly looked up doctor in the English-Greek translator my friend just gave me and realized Floyd wanted to take me to the doctor in the morning.

AMERICAN MILITARY BASE

At nine the next morning, Floyd came to get me with his military jeep. I could not walk, so Floyd scooped me up to carry me to the front seat of the jeep. Eleftherios still had no knowledge of Floyd, as he had not been at home when Floyd had come the night before and he always left early in the morning for work. However, it was difficult to hide an American jeep from the neighbors, whose curiosity caused them to look outside and see who it was that the American had come to see. I had to plead with my neighbors to not expose that Floyd was seeing me.

This was the first time I ever rode in a jeep. It was wonderful to see a star on the side of it instead of a swastika. There were only two seats, so Eleni could not come with me. As I rode to the American military base with Floyd, I was moved by his concern for me. I was grateful for the opportunity to see a doctor, as I was fearful of getting an infection that might result in me losing my leg. Until Floyd came to my rescue, I could only bandage my leg with rags to keep the flies out of the wound.

When we arrived at the military base a half-hour later, an American MP and a Greek police officer checked us in. As soon as we passed through the gates, Floyd took me directly to the doctor's office. Floyd carried me in and sat me on the examination table. The doctor, who was around thirty-five, was very polite. He carefully removed my bandages, cleaned the wound with hydrogen peroxide, and then spread some ointment on it and re-bandaged it. The doctor then recommended to Floyd that I should have a tetanus shot, which I did not understand until I saw the needle. Even though I did not understand the reason for the shot, I trusted that what the doctor was doing would benefit me.

While the doctor was attending to me, Floyd's captain walked in. Floyd had previously sought his captain's permission to bring me there for medical attention. Floyd introduced me to Captain Capetoluso who was from Louisiana. Do not ask me if he had a southern accent because I wouldn't have known the difference. The captain said something to Floyd, which I gathered was an instruction to bring me to the cafeteria for something to eat. As soon as were finished with the doctor, I thanked him in German, as I thought he would understand that more than Greek. Floyd lifted me into the jeep again and drove me to the cafeteria. Once we were inside, John, who was working in the kitchen, came out to greet us. The captain showed up again and told John to tell me that I was invited to come eat dinner with Floyd at the base every Sunday evening.

Before Floyd and I left, I asked John to explain to him that he could no longer come to my home at night. I told him that my brother did not allow men to come to the house. I explained that Eleni could be the liaison between us. In the weeks that followed, we met secretly, without my brothers' knowledge. Eleni was the messenger and John was the translator. Eleni would tell Floyd the time that he could come to get me on Sundays, when my brother would be out with his cart selling wares on the streets. When Eleftherios came home from work in the evening, he always went out with his friends. Therefore, as long as Floyd had me home by eight, I knew I was safe. Just in case, I had my neighbors prepared to wave a warning flag if my brother was coming. During those years, a young man was not allowed to come to a young woman's house unless he came with a relative and was ready to propose.

FIRST KISS

After Floyd took me to the doctor and we had lunch, he took me back home and the neighbors reappeared like the bird out of a coo-coo clock. I emphatically reminded them to keep the secrecy of Floyd's existence. Floyd gingerly carried me inside and gently set me down, and then softly planted a single kiss on my cheek with his warm lips. Maybe more would have followed but he had to quickly escape before Eleftherios arrived on the scene.

I put a stocking over my new bandages so that my brother would been not aware that I was given medical care. I also had to hide the extra ointment and bandages that the kind doctor had given me. I was to return in one week to have him check the progress of my healing. I still have a scar on my leg to this day. It would be three months before my brother would be made aware of the fact that Floyd and I were seeing each other.

Floyd was twenty-six years old and I was nineteen. Seeing him would create an entirely new life for me. When I first met Floyd I felt I an enormous happiness, the kind of encompassing joy that can occur only as a result of real love. I fell in love with a man who was totally foreign in every way. He did not understand me and I could not understand him. He had light hair and blue eyes and I had dark brown hair with brown eyes. He was tall, handsome, and the sort of person you feel comfortable being around.

He fell in love with me from the first moment he saw me. He hunted me like a hunter hunts a deer in the forest. John told me that Floyd did not have his mind at work. John explained, "One day he almost let the boiler at the base explode, as his mind was on the hands of the clock, anxiously awaiting for seven when he would be finished with his duty and finally be free to go see his sweetheart."

In the beginning, I was afraid and somewhat reserved, but as time went on, the attention he gave me and his tenderness surprised me. He was crazy about me and I began to draw closer to him. Little by little I learned English and it allowed me to see Floyd in a new light. He was good-hearted, responsive, very intelligent, and strong willed. When he said *I love you* I knew the words that he spoke were coming from his heart because of the expressive emotion on his face and the welling tears in his eyes.

Meeting Floyd created a feeling of happiness and excitement in me. Every meeting was precious to me, and time only brought us even closer together. I forgot everybody and everything else, and I saw that Floyd felt the same thing only, perhaps, in a greater way.

Floyd and I exchanged pictures

MY FIRST SUNDAY DINNER

It was arranged with Floyd (through Eleni) that he would come get me two Sundays after my first visit to the base. This was to be the first of many visits for special Sunday dinners at the military cafeteria. I was excitedly nervous about what the rendezvous would be like.

I took the time to make sure that I looked my best for this first Sunday visit with Floyd. I remember I wore a cotton turquoise colored dress with a garnet red and white polka dotted nylon scarf. It was early in November and the weather was now cool, so I wore a light green wool coat. My chestnut brown hair was down to my shoulders and perfectly curled toward my cheeks. I was ready to go! It seemed like forever as I gazed out the window, waiting to see my American prince pull up in his 'green horse' to carry me off. Finally, Floyd came as the neighbors dutifully peered out of their windows when he arrived. By this time my leg had healed to the point that I was able to walk to the jeep and Floyd braced me with his hand as I settled into my seat.

When Floyd and I arrived at the gate, the MP checked my permit while enviously looking at Floyd for the *goods* he was carrying in his jeep. He parked near the cafeteria door. When we entered there was a sudden hush over the thirty GIs who were already eating. I was the only woman in the room and I felt my face becoming warmly red as all eyes fell on me. I felt like a Cretan princess while Prince Floyd escorted me to one of the square linen covered tables that was waiting to be occupied. Once seated, we waited to be served by our Greek-American friend, John, who was in the kitchen. The captain came over and warmly welcomed me, asking, "Would you like a glass of *Ouzo* or *Metaxa* (Greek brandy)?" He smiled and told us, "As soon as you came in the guys asked me, 'Who's that beauty with Floyd?'" Soon afterward, John greeted us by bringing my first plate of American food from the kitchen: roast beef, mashed potatoes with gravy, and a salad, along with a perfect slice of pumpkin pie. After having meat rarely during the war, this dinner was a delicious, savory treat.

Captain Capetalouso made a special request of me through John, who had by now become our friend, not just our interpreter. John explained to me that the men would be celebrating an American holiday called Thanksgiving later that month. The captain explained that frozen turkeys would be coming from America by plane. John said, "The captain wants to know if you know someone who raises pigs?" I replied, "I know someone in the village of Arhanes, about thirty to forty-five minutes from Iraklion." The Captain then commissioned Floyd and I to procure a freshly butchered Cretan village pig for the American holiday.

A few days later, Floyd and I went to the village. The villager who owned pigs agreed to bring one early enough for us to prepare it for the celebration. He would bring it by horse and wagon, which would take him two hours, instead of the thirty to forty-five minutes by jeep. The captain had also requested that we get fruit, so we were ordered a crate of fresh green ladyfinger grapes to be delivered along with the Thanksgiving pig.

After Floyd and I said our goodbyes he took me back to town. I had Floyd drop me off at the *Tris Kamares* so that I could walk the rest of the way home in case my brother was there. In the weeks that followed, Sunday dinners at the military base became a weekly occurrence. Additionally, I would meet Floyd in the evenings at *Tris Kamares* where he would drop off John and the other Greek men who worked at the base.

One of the evenings that I met Floyd at the *Tris Kamares* it was a clear night and the full moon smiled down at us as we strolled along. Floyd and I sat down on one of the benches, eating warm roasted pumpkin seeds. While we were sitting there, he took my hand and said, "I would like you to come to America with me." I wasn't too sure what he was saying and I repeated, "America?" He said, "Yes, America." I didn't know if that meant he would be returning to America or if he was asking me to come to America.

The following Sunday at dinner, I saw John and said

to him, "Can you please ask Floyd to tell you what he was saying to me the other evening about America?" John asked Floyd and he replied with a smile on his face, "Tell her that I would like to take her to America with me." When John told me what Floyd said, I responded, "Please tell him that he has a great dream, but only time will tell if that is meant to be. My father is in Athens and I am only nineteen years old and traditionally it is proper to ask my father for his permission to marry his daughter. So I would like for him to go to Athens to meet my father." Floyd said that he would like to go to Athens but he would need permission to leave the base for the trip.

We continued our evening promenades and shortly thereafter, Floyd announced to me, "I have spoken to the captain and asked if I could take a week of leave to go to Athens to meet your father. He gave me his permission to go after Thanksgiving."

THREADS, THANKSGIVING, AND BLESSINGS

The night before the American Thanksgiving holiday, when my brother was out, Floyd came to the apartment. He hadn't been there very long before he said something to me that I did not quite understand. He wrote the words down and I found the translation in my dictionary. He wanted some thread. I laughed at him, and, perplexed, I asked what he would do with the thread. "Please give me some thread," he repeated. I thought he wanted to sew a button on his shirt. However, I looked at his shirt and none of the buttons were missing.

I gave him some thread and he in his persistent way told me to sit down. He took hold of my hand and measured my finger with it. Then he took some more thread from a spool in my sewing box and measured my waist and chest. He put the threads in his pocket. With a glint in his eye, he leaned down and gently kissed me saying, "I am going to have a great surprise for you."

Floyd also told me that evening, "I wrote to a friend at the base in Athens who is from Chicago and speaks Greek fluently. I asked if he could go with me to meet your father and act as our interpreter." Floyd had one request of me. "I would like you to write a letter to your father and explain to him why I am asking to meet with him. I will personally hand him the letter when I see him."

Thanksgiving finally arrived and Captain Capetaluso had invited the mayor of the city, the chief of the police department, and many dignitaries from the city for this special celebration. Among them were the attorney and his family whom I had worked for when I was fourteen. Floyd and I were seated together and when they spotted me they were dumbfounded and surprised to see their former maid sitting next to an American soldier, let alone among the city dignitaries. The last time I had seen the attorney was when I stopped working for them three years prior. The family approached us and I introduced them to Floyd. I explained to them that Floyd was courting me and that our intentions were to marry and that he was going to meet my father in Athens to receive his blessing.

Our first Thanksgiving dinner together consisted of turkey, cranberry jelly, mashed potatoes with gravy, salad, and pumpkin pie for desert. And don't forget the succulent Cretan village pig. That was delicious! At the end of the dinner the captain stood up and toasted everyone with a glass of wine, and then he gave a speech explaining the meaning of Thanksgiving to the Greek guests.

Floyd was set to leave the following Monday, so I

began to write a detailed letter to my father for Floyd to give to him. I told him how happy I was to have met a man who was so sincere, honest, and wonderful. I wrote that we planned to get married and that all I was asking him for was to give us his blessings. I gave Floyd the letter as soon as I was done. He received it and assured me that he would take it to my father. He left for Athens on a military plane on Monday morning.

When Floyd returned from meeting my father he was on cloud nine. He expressed how he had a wonderful time with my father, who treated him and his friend to dinner at a hotel. My father gave Floyd a letter to bring back to me. I translated it to Floyd as I read it, "Father says he enjoyed talking with you and we have his blessing to get married." Now we were both on cloud nine.

Floyd was determined to get going with our official papers so that we could get married. I told him that I would like to get married in the beautiful Cathedral of Saint Minas in Irakliaon, where I could have all of my relatives and friends around me. "I would like that too," Floyd said. "I will go to the American embassy tomorrow and get the papers started. I would like to get married in February, close to your birthday."

"That would be wonderful!" I exclaimed and gave him a big hug. He embraced me so tightly that I felt I could be in his arms forever. I felt so secure and confident when I was close to him.

I anxiously waited every day to see Floyd. He created new life in me and he made me feel so wonderful that I

would sing a new song to him every day. One of the songs
was called *Two Black Eyes*, but I changed it to blue because
his eyes were blue. The song went like this:

> *Two blue eyes drove me crazy one day,*
> *They mesmerized me,*
> *they took my heart away.*
> *Two little kisses he gave me upon my lips and*
> *Ever since then, I sing out every night;*
> *The eyes, the eyes that are yours,*
> *Your eyes that have such sweetness,*
> *I sincerely speak the truth to you,*
> *I do not desire anything, not even palaces,*
> *For me, the world is your two eyes.*

After getting permission from his captain to use the
jeep, Floyd came to get me for a trip to my birthplace, the
village of Mohos. In Mohos we would obtain my birth
certificate and other papers we needed to get married. We
planned to stop at my yiayia's village on the way.

The road going to Yiayia's village was deeply rutted and
very rough. The Germans had blown up some of the
bridges before they left Crete. There were signs of damage
all around to remind me that there had been a war going on
not very long ago. Floyd had to drive carefully so that we
would not fall into an abyss. As we traveled along this
rutted road we saw a villager walking. Floyd said, "Let's
stop and give him a ride if he is going in the same
direction." We stopped and I asked him if he would like to

ride with us. To my surprise, he was my father's first cousin, George. By the expression on his face I think he was more surprised than I was. We were both going to Yiayia's village, so he rode with us.

After a half-hour of splashing through the mud and deep potholes, we arrived at Yiayia's village in Avdou. As we entered the village, people followed us all the way to Yiayia's house. They all wondered what an American vehicle was doing in their community. We arrived at Yiayia's but she was not at home. Uncle George went to the neighbor's to look for her and before long, I spotted her walking toward us. Before she reached me, I ran up to her and gave her a big hug.

I couldn't hold my words for a single minute longer. "Yiayia," I said while still hugging her, "I am getting married to an American soldier. Come and I will introduce you. He is a wonderful man." She was very surprised, but also very happy for me. She gave us her blessings.

In no time the word got around the village. My aunts, Maria, Polymia, and Athena came and prepared a great dinner to celebrate our joyous news. After dinner, Floyd and I drove to my hometown. Children and grownups climbed onto the jeep to travel with us, some hanging on the fenders. Uncle George came along to direct us to the person we needed to see to obtain my papers. We acquired up the papers and returned to Iraklion. When we returned, we sent all the needed paperwork to the American embassy in Athens so that they could issue the correct documents that would allow us to marry.

Time went by and we did not hear from the American embassy for a long time. Then we received a telegram from the embassy, telling us that within three days a military plane would arrive in Iraklion. The documents would be with the captain flying the plane. We were excited to know that our papers would finally arrive. Our joy and excitement quickly turned to anguish and sorrow when Floyd and I learned that the plane did not make it. The aircraft encountered mechanical problems and crashed into the Mediterranean Sea with soldiers on board. All of them drowned. Our papers were lost with them. I was eating dinner with Floyd at the military base when he told me and he promised to go have the paperwork started again. I was so stricken and my tears could not be contained. I was so grieved that the men had died. Our papers could be obtained again, but the men were gone forever. This was a very sad Sunday dinner indeed.

HOLY THEOPHANY

Christmas came and went and it was the feast of Epiphany. Floyd came early that morning and asked me if we could go to church together. I told him I'd like to go because that day is a special day of the Lord and we could receive a special blessing from the priest. We walked to Saint Titus church. As we entered to light our candles, the candle keeper directed us to our seats. Floyd was surprised when he was directed to the right side of the church where all the men were standing and I was directed to the left where all the women sat. When the service was over I asked the priest if he could come to bless my apartment. He said he would be over around one.

I asked Floyd if he could stay for the blessing. He said that he had the day off so he could. When the priest came to bless the house my friend, Amalia, who lived across the street, brought us a platter full of *meloumakarna* and a pot of tea. I invited my neighbors and friends over for the blessing service. While the priest was performing the service, my brother Eleftherios unexpectedly showed

270

up.

He saw all the neighbors and wondered what was going on. Then he saw Floyd for the first time. He was really surprised. When the priest left, I introduced my brother to Floyd. My brother said to me, "What is this American doing here?" One of the neighbors piped up and said, "Can't you see your sister will soon get married to this American man. You almost crippled her when you hit her in the leg. You should get down on your knees and apologize to her."

My brother turned around, looked me in the eyes and said, "I am really sorry for the pain I caused you. However, that the scar you have on your leg should always remind you that I wanted to protect you from gossip and embarrassment. As your brother, I care for you and love you dearly." He then reached up to Floyd and gave him a big hug saying, "Welcome to our family." While I was interpreting what my brother was saying to Floyd, we all had tears in our eyes. From that point on, Floyd and I ceased meeting secretly and the reality of his presence in our lives slowly became real for my brother.

FLOYD'S SUPRISE

I had forgotten all about the surprise Floyd had promised me three months earlier. It was a cold, crisp sunny day in January of 1946 when Floyd came to see me, carrying a large wooden box from America. He had a huge smile on his face. No sooner had Floyd walked into the house than my neighbors and friends came knocking on the door. They had seen Floyd carry the sturdy box. My neighbors came in saying, "You do not mind if we come in and see what he got for you, do you?" Despite how careful we had been, word got around about us seeing each other. Everyone wanted to join us in our happiness.

I thought that it must be some shoes from the base. I could hardly wait to see what he had brought for me. Floyd began to open the parcel. First, he pulled out a pair of shoes, then a silk slip and underwear. After that, he unfurled a gorgeous wedding dress that had a beautiful veil flowing from a crown decorated with rhinestones. He carefully opened a small silver box and handed it to me. Inside were the most beautiful rings I had ever seen. My hands trembled and I almost dropped to the floor. I could not believe what I was seeing. I was in dazed speechlessness as Floyd put the ring on my shaky hand. I reached to hug him and kiss him on the cheek.

Floyd hugged me and said, "I love you with all my heart and soul, and as soon as our papers arrive we will get married. I promise I will try to make you happy." As soon as I could speak again, I translated the words to all my friends. We all jumped up and down, hugging each other with tears in our eyes.

FLIGHT TO ATHENS

It was March 1946 when Floyd told me that his entire company was being transferred to Athens. I was shocked. I asked him, "What will happen to me?"

"What do you mean? You are coming with me. Wherever I go, you are coming with me!" I will not go without you and that is a promise. You understand?" I nodded my head in acknowledgement. "Just get ready," he said. "Pack your things so we can take off in a moment's notice. In the meantime, have your brother take a ship to Athens. Your father can be notified to meet him at the port." After the Germans evacuated Iraklion, my father came from the village to see my brother and I. He told us that he had a letter from a friend who lived in Athens. His friend invited him to come there to start a small business together. He accepted the offer that is how my father was already in Athens ahead of us. I told Floyd, "I will call my father to let him know when Eleftherios will be there."

After a day or so, Floyd informed me that we had a week to get ready for the flight to Athens. I immediately sent a message to Uncle George to build me a trunk for my belongings. He had less than one week to build it. My uncle brought the trunk just in time. It was all varnished and polished. It looked beautiful, ready for it's long journey ahead! In fact, that trunk has a history, as I brought it all the way to America. Many years later, my oldest son, Tony, went to visit Eleftherios in Crete and met my Uncle George, who had a lot of fun telling Tony how fast he had to build that trunk to have it ready for me so I didn't miss the flight to Athens.

A week later, Floyd came and told me that his captain had given him permission for me to join them on the military flight to Athens. Floyd loaded my new trunk into the jeep in no time. We said goodbye to my neighbors, whom I promised to write to as soon as I arrived in Athens. It was an emotional departure for us all.

Floyd and I took off for the airport. I was so excited for my first ride in an airplane and it was an American military plane at that! When we arrived, the men from Floyd's company had already boarded the plane. One of the military men loaded my trunk, while Floyd guided me onto the airplane. I was the only girl on a plane with thirty soldiers. As soon as we entered the aircraft, all eyes were glued on me. I was the central attraction and I truly felt like a princess! It was always that way whenever Floyd and I were together. The men were surprised to see a civilian passenger on the plane. Perhaps they were wondering who this lucky guy was who had the privilege of having his fiancé with him. I was amused, but I pretended not to notice anything.

It took a little over one hour to get to Athens from Iraklion. However, with all eyes looking at me, I thought that the flight would never end. When we finally landed at the airport, the air was warm and there was a gentle breeze coming from the sea. When we exited the plane, Floyd asked the port official to borrow a car to take me to the hotel where my father had rented a suite.

We arrived at the hotel to find my father broiling fish that had been caught that day. He invited us to stay and I made a delicious salad and french fries to supplement the meal. Floyd would come from the military base almost every evening to visit us at the hotel. We spent several weekends together. We strolled along the avenues of Athens, window-shopping and visiting museums, churches, and stores selling arts and crafts. The Acropolis was one of Floyd's favorite places to visit, and he took numerous pictures of me standing at the statue of Athena.

While we stayed in Athens, Floyd and I had the opportunity to visit the Battle Ship Missouri. The peace treaty with Japan was signed on this ship. The ship was touring many ports to proclaim the defeat of Japan and the end of the Second World War.

THE WEDDING

Floyd ordered a limousine to take us to the church to get married. I waited at the front of the hotel. When he arrived he helped me into the back seat and sat next to me. He put his arm around and said, "Finally, we're getting married today." My father and brother, who had already gone ahead of us, were waiting in front of the church when we arrived. Floyd opened the door of the limousine, holding the back of my wedding dress so that it would not touch the ground. He gently walked me to where my father was standing.

In the Orthodox Church, when a couple gets married they have a sponsor who participates in the sacrament. It is much like a godparent who sponsors a person being baptized. This person is called, *koumbaro*. It is like a best man or maid of honor, but the relationship is even deeper. They become like family and spiritually speaking the *koumbaro* is supports the marriage of the couple. Of course when you are thousands of miles away, this becomes a little difficult. My father's friend and new business partner,

Pavlos, offered to be our *koumbaro*. He had lived in America before and could speak and read English.

Pavlos came out of the church to greet us and then he accompanied Floyd to the altar where the priest was waiting. My two cousins and their husbands were sitting in the front pews, where my brother joined them. The ceremony began with the chanter.

I was dressed in the beautiful white wedding gown that Floyd had ordered from America. As my father slowly walked me down the aisle, I was overwhelmed. It was difficult to believe what was happening, it was like a dream. I suddenly realized that it was all truly real. I looked down the aisle and saw Floyd standing there in a new suit, tall and slim. He looked so handsome. How funny, I thought, how God's plan brought us together: two people from distance lands.

My father walked me to where Floyd was standing. While the priest performed the ceremony, I trembled all over. After the wedding ceremony was over, the priest's wife invited us all for a small reception at their house. It was very gracious of her to offer us a wonderful lamb roast with all the trimmings. She was very pleased to do it, since I was far away from home and most of my relatives and friends were in Crete and could not attend the wedding.

While we were eating, Floyd mentioned that we would get married again that evening. I was very surprised. "We are only half married," he said. I thought he was joking. I said, "We just got married!" Floyd said, "Yes, I am married to you, but according to United States law, you are not married to me until we get married with a USA minister and the American ambassador signs our marriage certificate." I then realized he was serious. So we took a taxi to the Baptist minister's house that evening. The captain and the American ambassador were present. It was a short but lovely ceremony. The ambassador signed our marriage certificate.

The captain brought a platter of hors d'oeuvres and a bottle of champagne. He toasted us and wished us long and lasting happiness. As we sat there eating the delicious appetizers and sipping the champagne, the captain told the story of how Floyd brought me to the base to see the doctor who treated the wound on my leg. He said, "I think that wound brought Aristea and Floyd together." He then pointed to my leg where I still have the mark.

Courage For Survival

Floyd and I married in Athens in 1946. The priest's wife gave us a small reception.

281

DEPARTING FOR ITALY

Floyd was transferred from Athens to Italy four days after out wedding. My father, brother, and I accompanied Floyd to the airport. It was May if 1946 and after the cold winter, the warm sun felt good on my body. Floyd noticed the sadness on my face. He reassured me saying, "Don't worry, honey, I promise I will write to let you know how things are going as soon I arrive in Italy. The first and most important thing is for me to go to the head office at the military base to inquire about the necessary papers for your passage to Italy. That way I can send them to you so you can come to Italy as soon as possible."

When we arrived at the airport the military plane was already boarding the men. Floyd kissed me for the last time, and as he boarded the plane I felt as though he would be gone forever. I waved goodbye at the plane as it took off down the runway and watched it disappear in moments. The three of us returned to the hotel and I felt as though part of my soul had left me.

The days went by so slowly, like a snail going down a

mile long track. I anxiously longed for Floyd's first letter, which felt like it would never come. Finally, when I received his letter, my heart seemed to beat a hundred beats a second. I opened it immediately. However, I realized that I could not read it, as I could not yet read English. I had to wait for our *koumbaro*, Paul, who knew how to read English, to translate it for me. I called Paul to come for dinner at the hotel and when he came the first thing he did was read the letter from Floyd. It was such a great joy to hear him say that he loved me.

> *I think of you every day and I long for your love. I want to hear your voice, to see you next to me, and feel your warmth. I'm working diligently to obtain your travel documents so you can come to me soon. In a few days I should have some news from the government office. I love you and I miss you very much. I hope to get together soon!*
> *Your loving husband,*
> *Floyd*

My impatience while waiting to hear from Floyd was like lava brewing inside a volcano, I thought would erupt at any moment. A few days later, I received a letter from the American embassy saying that my authorization papers had come, allowing me to depart for Italy. I was filled with of ecstasy when I received the news, and a great sigh of relief burst forth. On the way to Italy I was to be accompanied by Miss Frances, an American military escort. She would later escort me all the way from Italy to America.

A couple days later, Miss Frances called me at the hotel and said that she would have a limousine pick me up early the next morning to take me to the airport. When the limousine came the next morning, my father and my brother came with me to the military airport. We met Miss Frances. She was very young and was beautifully dressed in a military uniform. She introduced herself as my escort and told me that she would help me with everything I needed.

Before we boarded the American military plane, I hugged Father and Eleftherios, and tears came down our cheeks as we said goodbye. At that moment, we realized that we would not see each other for a long time, if ever.

We arrived at the airport in Naples after a three hours flight. There was a small group of people waiting, but I didn't see Floyd anywhere. I was disappointed that he was not at the airport to meet me and I began to worry that I would not find him at all. Miss Frances suggested that we go to an information desk to inquire where we might find Floyd. I showed the man my papers and the letter I had received from Floyd. The man read the return address and said that according to the address on the envelope, Floyd was stationed in Rome. Miss Frances called a taxi that took us to the military base in Naples for lunch. In meantime, the taxi driver took my luggage to the hotel where I was to stay with other war brides.

After lunch, we went outside and I saw a captain. He was waiting for his chauffer to come. I asked him, "Are you going to town? I would like it if I could ride with you to a telegram office, as I would like to send a message to my husband in Rome." He replied, "I would be more than glad to take you. In fact, I am going there myself to send a message to my wife." I hopped into the limousine and in a short time we were there. I sent a message to Floyd:

I am in Naples, and I was very disappointed when I had found out that you are not stationed here. I miss you and I feel very lonely without you being here. I love you and I hope to see you soon.
Your loving wife,
Aristea

I thanked the captain for taking me to town to send the telegram to Floyd. While we were waiting for the chauffer to come, the captain offered to buy me an ice cream nearby. We talked for a long time. He told me he was from Omaha, Nebraska and he was making his military career permanent. I told him I was a war bride going to America. After a while, the chauffer came and drove us back to the base. The captain said goodbye and wished me a safe trip to America.

It was early afternoon with a bright, blue sky overhead. The hotel was only a few blocks away from the base. As I walked along the road, I noticed that greenery and blooming flowers surrounded many of the homes. The hotel we stayed in had many accommodations, including a beauty salon, nail trimming, laundry, and room services.

I soon discovered that there were two families from Greece staying on the same floor and we became good friends. They asked me to help them because I spoke English better than them. The Red Cross appointed me to translate for them when they needed examinations or shots, so I volunteered whenever they needed me.

While staying in Naples, Italy, I met other Greek ladies and their children bound for America. The Red Cross appointed me to help them with obtaining their shots, medical supplies, and oral translation from English to Greek

On a Friday morning, three days after I arrived in Naples, a porter from the hotel knocked at my door. "Mrs. Pettis, someone is waiting downstairs. They want to see you," he announced. I immediately jumped out of my bed, put my white dress on, and hurried downstairs. I saw Floyd from the top the stairs and I ran into his arms. He hugged me and lifted me right off the floor, but when he saw that I had lipstick on my lips he only kissed me on the cheek. Sophia, the Greek lady who stayed in the room next door, had asked me the day before to go shopping in town. When she was putting lipstick on, she turned to me and said, "Here put some on. You will look better." That was the first time in my life that I had put any makeup on my face.

Floyd was in shock to see me looking that way! He said, "Get ready, we are going to the base for breakfast. And please wash that lipstick off your lips!" After that, many years passed before I tried lipstick again.

As we walked to the base for breakfast, we went down the main avenue to look for a hotel to stay in. After a short while we saw a sign that said, *Bed and Breakfast, Family Owned.* We stopped and rang the doorbell. An older gentleman opened the door and next to him was his wife, who had a bright smile on her face. They introduced themselves. Her name was Seniora Elena and his name was Senior Roberto.

After we introduced ourselves, they invited us in to look at the room. It was a nice clean room with a queen sized bed and lots of windows with a beautiful view of the sea. We said that we would take the room and paid them for three days. The accommodations were very good and the breakfast was tasty. Every morning they served us omelets, fresh baked bread, jam, butter, and fresh fruit.

To welcome us on the first day, Senora Elena invited us down to the small dinette area where she had a plate of appetizers and another plate full of fresh cherries from her tree in the backyard. Floyd was so happy, he put his arms around me and kissed me saying, "Now I can enjoy kissing you since you took that lipstick off your lips." I kissed him and I said, "I cannot believe that I am here with you in this room." It was like a dream that I wished would never end. We spent three wonderful days together. It was like a second honeymoon. We visited museums and learned about the city of Naples and the impressive volcano, Mount Vesuvius, which loomed in the distance.

The weather was warm during the first week of June. We enjoyed going to the beach every afternoon and then later on we would go to the military base for dinner. The days went by too quickly. Floyd had to return to Rome. He had to travel back to America with the military, and I had to travel separately on a ship with other war brides. I accompanied Floyd to the train station, where he would take the train back to Rome. He kissed me and told me he'd see me in America in July. He waved goodbye as the train left the station. My heart sunk as he left me again, but I knew that we were on the way to begin our lives together in America.

EPILOGUE

After my mother died, my life changed drastically. I had to face the challenges and uncertainties of making a living for myself at ten years of age. With great determination, faith, and courage, I was on my way to face the world. I was fortunate that most of the people who I worked for allowed me to attend school. I knew back then, that in order to succeed in life I had to get a good education. I took this seriously and studied very hard. I was gifted in learning foreign languages. I took German and French in school, and when it came time to learn English later in my life, I taught myself how to speak and write.

In the end, all the hardships I endured developed into a life I could never have dreamed of. That was when I met Floyd. The unfortunate life I went through during the war is behind me now. The life I went through made me strong enough to know how to survive in any situation. I know my faith in God gave me the strength and hope to face any future tragedies and challenges with courage.

ABOUT THE AUTHOR

From a child of war in her beloved Greece, to a war bride in America, to homesteading in Alaska, Aristea Vasiloyanakis Pettis has lived a remarkable life— a life sustained by her deep and abiding faith. Aristea is a mother of four and grandmother of six. She has lived in San Jose, California since 1962 and is an active member of Saint Basil Greek Orthodox Church and founding member of the Golden Seniors of Saint Nicholas Greek Orthodox Church. Her many interests include charitable works, local politics, gardening, and cooking. In 2003 she published her first book, *Yiayia's Kouzina*.

Made in the USA
San Bernardino, CA
29 December 2013